Shaped by the Standards

# Shaped by the Standards

## Geographic Literacy Through Children's Literature

Linda K. Rogers

**Through Children's Literature**

Teacher **Ideas** Press

An imprint of Libraries Unlimited

Westport, Connecticut • London

**Library of Congress Cataloging-in-Publication Data**

Rogers, Linda K., 1947–
    Shaped by the standards : geographic literacy through children's literature / Linda K. Rogers.
        p. cm. — (Through children's literature)
    Includes bibliographical references and index.
    ISBN 978–1–59158–462–9 (alk. paper)
    1. Geography—Study and teaching (Elementary)   2. Children's literature—
Study and teaching (Elementary)   I. Title.
  G73.R76 2008
    372.89'1—dc22        2008000423

British Library Cataloguing in Publication Data is available.

Library of Congress Catalog Card Number: 2008000423
ISBN: 978–1–59158–462–9

First published in 2008

Libraries Unlimited/Teacher Ideas Press, 88 Post Road West, Westport, CT 06881
A Member of the Greenwood Publishing Group, Inc.
www.lu.com

Printed in the United States of America

The paper used in this book complies with the
Permanent Paper Standard issued by the National
Information Standards Organization (Z39.48–1984).

10 9 8 7 6 5 4 3 2 1

# Contents

## CHAPTER 3—
## PHYSICAL SYSTEMS

## CHAPTER 4—
## HUMAN SYSTEMS

## CHAPTER 5—
## ENVIRONMENT AND SOCIETY

## CHAPTER 6—
## THE USES OF GEOGRAPHY

# Acknowledgments

Love and thanks to Jack who is always there for me. Special thanks to Kathy Boyle, Lauren Deery, Anne Miller, Shawn Norris, Pat Pinciotti, and Amy Pinkerton who shared their ideas and creativity.

# Introduction

For more than a decade I have been intrigued by geographic literacy and the rich assortment of children's literature available to support students' geographic learning. I teach a social studies methodology course as part of an undergraduate teacher preparation program. My students are always amazed to discover that geography is more than place-names and location, and they love the children's literature they encounter and use to teach geographic concepts in their classroom placements. They often become as excited as their elementary students when they rediscover the world through their eyes—especially when presented with an excellent piece of children's literature.

The purpose of this book is to engage teachers in looking at the world and geography in new and exciting ways. I want to send you out to your school and community libraries asking for the many wonderful books available. But, most of all, I want you to be inspired to *regularly* teach the whole of geography, not just map skills. Creating geographically literate students is creating knowledgeable world citizens.

> Ability to locate words in a dictionary does not make a person literate. Literacy begins when one is able to understand the meanings of words, employ them in coherent sentences and paragraphs, and understand clearly the meanings of these word combinations when reading them. . . . Thus geographical literacy is attained only when people understand why places are where they are, what these places are like, and how they relate to these people and to other places. (Natoli & Gritzner, 1988, p. 2)

As you read this book, notice the number of places where geographic concepts cross over into the science concepts you teach in your classroom. Being aware of commonalities in multiple subject areas allows us to integrate curriculum and helps us to assist our students in making meaningful connections between learning and their everyday lives.

## The National Geography Standards

In response to the report, *A Nation at Risk: The Imperative for Educational Reform* (National Commission on Excellence in Education), published in 1983, the geographic community gathered to determine what could be done to improve geographic education across the country. During the next decade, geographers worked with educators and parents to create a program to improve their understanding of what geography entails. Summer workshops trained teachers who returned to their communities to teach other teachers. A network of geographic literacy grew across the country and each state established a Geographic Alliance to support geographic education.

*Geography for Life: National Geography Standards* (National Council for the Social Studies) was published in 1994. Rich in content, this document outlines 18 Standards organized within Six Essential Elements. There are benchmarks at grades 4, 8, and 12. For those of us who use the Five Fundamental Themes of Geography (Location, Place, Human/Environmental Interaction, Movement, and Regions) (Kimball, 1987, p. 3) to organize our thoughts and plans for teaching geographic content, we can see the intersection of the five themes in the titles and content of the Six Essential Elements.

---

### The Five Themes

**LOCATION: Position on the Earth's Surface**
Absolute and relative location are two ways of describing the positions of people and places on the earth's surface.

**PLACE: Physical and Human Characteristics**
All places on the earth have distinctive tangible and intangible characteristics that give them meaning and character and distinguish them from other places.

**RELATIONSHIPS WITHIN PLACES: Humans and Environments**
All places on the earth have advantages and disadvantages for human settlement.

**MOVEMENT: Humans Interacting on the Earth**
Human beings occupy places unevenly across the face of the earth. Yet these people interact with each other: that is, they travel from one place to another, they communicate with each other or they relay upon products, information, and ideas that come from beyond their immediate environment.

**REGIONS: How They Form and Change**
The basic unit of geographic study is the region, an area that displays unity in terms of a selected criteria.

---

**Five Fundamental Themes of Geography (Kemball, 1987, p. 3).**

## Using This Book

This book uses the Six Essential Elements to organize the chapters. Within each chapter is a brief discussion of the standards, with reference to the themes, organized under the essential element. Following the standards' benchmarks, the focus of this book is grades K–4. Sample lesson plans in each chapter provide models for instruction, offering ideas that can be used at several levels. Remember that the standards listed at the beginning of each chapter reflect what the students *should know and understand at the end of the fourth grade*.

## Lesson Plans

The lesson plans are designed for various levels of understanding. They have a grade level designation, but good teachers are continually adapting and adopting good ideas and strategies to meet the needs of their students. Examine your state or district curriculum and adapt or adopt the lesson plans to meet your students' needs. Because the lesson plans include the use of a particular book or relate to a text set cited in the chapter, it is important for the reader to know that there is *not* a children's picture or nonfiction book for every standard. These plans and text sets are a beginning place, and I hope they trigger new ideas. As you use these ideas and text sets, make notes in the margins about new books or other ways to teach the lesson to meet the learning goal.

## Best Practices and Exemplary Strategies

If you read the *Geography for Life* descriptions of students who at the end of fourth grade are "aspiring to standard" (p. 224–226), you will note as I have that some of these problems relate to limited academic proficiencies, and others relate to cognitive development. Some students are not yet able to fully understand the abstract concepts introduced. Therefore it is essential that teachers provide concrete ways to present these abstract ideas to begin building a knowledge base. The lesson plans and teaching ideas include graphic organizers and other supporting materials to actively engage the students in the learning activity.

## Text Sets

At the beginning of each chapter you will find several text sets, a discussion about how they were assembled, and suggestions on how I would use the books. My definition of a text set is a thoughtful collection of children's literature—both fact and fiction—that can be used to teach a particular concept. The set should provide multiple reading levels and points of view so that students can read independently, as well as be engaged in read-aloud experiences with the teacher. The content should encourage students to think and explore the content with the teacher and their peers. At a time when many districts are not purchasing social studies textbooks, the task falls to the classroom teacher—with the assistance and support of the school librarian—to gather books and other resources to teach curriculum well and enthusiastically. Be forewarned! You may find the same book in more than one text set. Some books such as *A River Ran Wild* by Lynne Cherry (1992) can teach two very different lessons.

My goal was to provide the most recently published books. That does not mean that older books are not valuable sources. Many of my favorites are more than a decade old and still hold true in terms of content and student interest. When you gather text sets, do not be afraid to add older titles *if* they meet your requirements for the content of the unit of study.

## The Annotated Bibliography

I have been collecting children's literature titles using the Five Fundamental Themes of Geography as my marker for nearly 15 years, and I have broadened my list as I have taught a social studies methods course. The books in the annotated bibliography are listed in text sets within the six chapters. The chapter and text set title are indicated at the end of each entry.

I have purchased many of my favorite books so that they are always available as I teach methods courses. I also borrow books regularly from my community library that I share with students. Looking over the list of books in the bibliography, I realize the collection reflects my areas of interest. You will see lots of books by authors I find to be geography/social studies writers—regardless of whether they are intentionally so—including Eve Bunting, Lynne Cherry, Gail Gibbons, Cheryl Harness, Ted Lewin, Patricia Polacco, Allen Say, and Jane Yolen.

I love the informative alphabet books by Jerry Pallotta, the more recent ones from Lynne Cheney, and the incredible series that Sleeping Bear Press is now publishing about states and cities. In fact, research indicates that reluctant readers are often enticed by informational books, so I am looking closely at those beautiful nonfiction books growing in numbers in children's libraries' collections.

So, how can you find the books referred to in the chapters? There are three sections in the Annotated Bibliography: Children's Literature, Classroom Reference, or Informational Books, and Teacher Resources. The Children's Literature selections are more heavily narrative picture books that tell a story. Some are fictionalized true stories and some are the more traditional information books. I made the decision to include them in this section based on whether I would use them as a classroom read-aloud book.

The Classroom Reference or Informational Books section includes nonfiction books that are part of a series, traditional informational books that do not lend themselves to a read-aloud experience but would be great books to pull out and read a page or portion of in class, and books like Lynne Cheney's *Our 50 States: A Family Adventure Across America* (2006).

The last section, Teacher Resources, is for the teacher's information. Most of the books are actually intended for a student audience. This book is focused on kindergarten to fourth-grade classrooms; some of the books included in this section are too sophisticated for that range of students, or the content does not really match the standards, so I have included them here as teacher resources. They are excellent books to build background knowledge, and teachers need to continually update what they know.

## A Final Word

At the end of the semester our faculty team provides a bag of mementos to our cohort of students heading out to student teach. Each offers a bit of wisdom to accompany the selected memento for the course. For social studies I include a votive candle and tell them, "Allow your knowledge of the world and its people to illuminate your teaching." I charge you to do the same!

# References

Cheney, Lynne. (2006). *Our 50 States: A Family Adventure Across America.* New York: Simon and Schuster.

Cherry, Lynne. (1992). *A River Ran Wild.* San Diego: A Gulliver Green Book.

*Geography for Life: The National Geography Standards.* (1994). Washington, D.C.: National Council for the Social Studies.

Kemball, Walter G. (1987). *K–6 Geography: Themes, Key Ideas, and Learning Opportunities.* Washington, D.C.: National Geographic Society.

National Commission on Excellence in Education. (1983). *A Nation at Risk: The Imperative for Educational Reform.* Washington, D.C.: U.S. Department of Education.

Natoli, Salvatore J., & Gritzner, Charles F. (1988). Modern Geography in *Strengthening Geography in the Social Studies.* Bulletin No. 81. Washington, D.C.: National Council for the Social Studies.

## *Suggested Reading*

Barrentine, S. J. (1996). Engaging with Reading Through Interactive Read-Alouds. *The Reading Teacher, 50*(1), 36–43.

## CHAPTER 1

# The World in Spatial Terms

Physical and human phenomena are spatially distributed over Earth's surface. The outcome of *Geography for Life: National Geography Standards* (National Council for the Social Studies, 1994) is a geographically informed person (1) who sees meaning in the arrangement of things in space; (2) who sees relationships between people, places, and environments; (3) who uses geographic skills; and (4) who applies spatial and ecological perspectives to life situations.

## THE WORLD IN SPATIAL TERMS

Geography studies the relationships between people, places, and environments by making information about them into a spatial context.

The geographically informed person knows and understands:

1. How to use maps and other geographic representations, tools, and technologies to acquire, process, and report information from a spatial perspective, including:
   a. the characteristics and purposes of geographic representations such as maps, globes, graphs, diagrams, aerial and other photographs, and satellite-produced images;
   b. the characteristics and purposes of tools and technologies such as reference works and computer-based geographic information systems;
   c. how to display spatial information on maps and other geographic representations; and
   d. how to use appropriate geographic tools and technologies.

2. How to use mental maps to organize information about people, places, and environments in a spatial context, including:
   a. the locations of places within the local community and in nearby communities;
   b. the location of Earth's continents and oceans in relation to each other and to principal parallels and meridians; and
   c. the location of major physical and human features in the United States and on Earth.

3. How to analyze the spatial organization of people, places, and environments on Earth's surface, including:
   a. the spatial elements of point, line, area, and volume;
   b. the spatial concepts of location, distance, direction, scale, movement, and region;
   c. that places and features are distributed spatially across Earth's surface; and
   d. the causes and consequences of spatial interactions on Earth's surface.

---

*Geography for Life: National Geography Standards* (National Council for Social Studies, 1994, pp. 34, 106–112).

When you examine the performance expectations for the World in Spatial Terms, you will see the elements of the theme of Location and a touch of the theme of Place in Standard 3.

From kindergarten through fourth grade, students should have many opportunities to interact with geographic representations such as maps, globes, graphs, diagrams, aerial and other photographs, and satellite-produced images. They need to be able to create and use mental maps for academic and personal purposes. Educators know that modeling is powerful, so use the maps and globes in the classroom all the time. Find the setting of a book or identify the location of a current news story on a state, country, or world map. Show the weather map in the local newspaper so that students can compare their weather with the weather across the country.

When a question arises about how to move from one place to another, model your own mental map. Draw a quick map on the board and describe the directions visually and verbally. One kindergarten teacher regularly encourages her students to create mental maps. When they line up to leave the classroom for any reason, she says, "We are going to Art (or Music or lunch); should we turn right or left?" These questions continue throughout the trip to the classroom.

## Text Sets—Creating Maps, Atlases

The text sets in this chapter support learning the basic geographic terms and concepts related to creating and using maps. *Me on the Map* (Sweeney, 1998) and *Mapping Penny's World* (Leedy, 2000) are "faction books" in that they tell fictional stories as they impart factual information. The same book can be used several times during a unit of study while focusing on different concepts.

Allow third- and fourth-grade students to apply their map-reading skills using *The Once Upon a Time Map Book: Take a Tour of Six Enchanted Lands* (Hennessy, 1999), which is an atlas of fictional lands. Students can explore the six fictional lands and then apply Hennessy's technique as they create maps of fictional settings of their own choosing.

*Map Mania: Discovering Where You Are and Getting to Where You Aren't* (DiSpezio, 2002) is an informational book for students, and *Mapping the World* (Johnson, 1999) provides teachers with background information about the history of mapping. Ask your school librarian for suggestions on more titles.

All of the texts in the atlas section are informational. In addition, find a road atlas of the United States and Canada for use as a classroom reference. Refer to it as students read or discuss various settings in books or places where they travel. Help them build a natural curiosity about their world and practice their skills at the same time.

### Creating Maps

- DiSpezio, Michael A. (2002). *Map Mania: Discovering Where You Are and Getting to Where You Aren't*. New York: Sterling Publishing.

- Hennessy, B. G. (1999). *The Once Upon a Time Map Book: Take a Tour of Six Enchanted Lands*. Cambridge, MA: Candlewick Press.
- Johnson, S. A. (1999). *Mapping the World*. New York: Atheneum Books for Young Readers.
- Leedy, L. (2000). *Mapping Penny's World*. New York: Scholastic.
- Sweeney, J. (1998). *Me on the Map*. New York: Crown Publishers.

## *Atlases*

- Brooks, F. (1999). *The Usborne First Encyclopedia of Our World*. New York: Scholastic.
- Kapp, B. M. (2006). *Our World: A Child's First Picture Atlas*. Washington, D.C.: National Geographic Society.
- Mappin, J. (2004). *The Seven Continents of the World Jigsaw Book*. Victoria Australia: The Five Pile Press.
- Petty, K. (2000). *The Amazing Pop-Up Geography Book*. New York: Dutton Children's Books.

# Teaching Ideas—Lesson Plans and Extension/Application Activities

Before writing this book, I took a sabbatical from my university responsibilities to teach with my daughter Sarah and my son-in-law Chris. In both classrooms I taught geographic content. For Sarah's first-grade curriculum, the geographic concepts were identified and located in her district's curriculum map under social studies. In Chris's third-grade curriculum, some of the geographic concepts were situated in his district's curriculum map under social studies, and others were under science.

The following is an introductory lesson from Sarah's first-grade class. She works closely with a colleague, Jan, who also graciously allowed me to teach each lesson in her classroom.

## *Lesson Plan 1.1—Making Maps*

### LEVEL: KINDERGARTEN AND GRADE 1

### Learning Goals

- Students will create a three-dimensional representation of the classroom.
- Students will create a two-dimensional representation of the classroom.

### Assessment

- Informal assessment: Discussion while whole class creates three-dimensional block map and two-dimensional map on an overhead transparency.
- Informal assessment: Anecdotal notes as each student identifies the location of his/her desk on the two-dimensional map on overhead transparency.
- Formal assessment possibilities:
  - map from Extension Activity 1.1

    ✓+   map has three added elements that also appear in the legend

    ✓    map has fewer than three added elements that appear in the legend

    ✓−   map has fewer than three added elements or new elements that do not appear in the legend

  - map from Extension Activity 1.2 (See preceding rubric.)

### Materials

- *Me on the Map* (Sweeney, 1998).
- Building blocks: enough to represent the outside walls of the classroom in correct proportion. (Prepace the classroom to determine the general shape and dimensions. During the lesson tell the students that one block is used for each pace.)
- Overhead projector, transparency sheet, and pens.

### Key Questions and/or Vocabulary

- Map: a drawing that shows what places look like from above and where they are located
- Map legend or map key: a list of descriptions used on a map that tells what each symbol means.

### Procedure

#### *Motivation and Explanation*

- Gather the students on the floor.
- Ask students to define the term *map*. After allowing some discussion, tell students they are going to hear a book about a girl who makes numerous maps that show where she is located.
- Read *Me on the Map* (Sweeney, 1998), showing the illustrations. Make the read-aloud interactive by asking questions to guide thinking and accepting comments and questions as time allows. (For those not familiar with this strategy, read Shelby Barrentine's article, "Engaging with Reading Through Interactive Read-Alouds," in

the September 1996 issue of *The Reading Teacher*. Your school librarian can locate a copy for you.)

### Demonstration and Modeling

- Read the book and tell the students that you plan to create a map of the classroom using building blocks. Move the students to create a space in the center of the group for the block map. Make certain that everyone can see the process.
- Using a think-aloud strategy, identify the general characteristics of the room that will be used to create the three-dimensional map: major walls, comparison of length and width, windows, and doors.

  - Demonstrate using your pace as a nonstandard unit to measure the length and width of the classroom; have the students count with you as you pace off the distances.
  - Use the paces for length and width to determine the shape the classroom will be: square, rectangle, other.

- Use the blocks to begin to build the map of the classroom.

  - Think aloud about the shape and ask the students whether the wall with the bulletin board (for instance) should be longer, shorter, or the same as the wall that is perpendicular to it.
  - Based on student input, build two walls (single layer of blocks) to represent the front and one side wall. Ask the students for advice about the size of the other two walls.

- Lead a discussion with the students about the location of the doors and windows in the classroom and find those locations on the block walls. The classroom may have other structural features that can be identified such as a closet or bathroom. Decide whether to include these features in the discussion based on your students' abilities or the time you have for the lesson.

### Guided Practice

- Have students return to their seats; move to the overhead projector at the front of the room.
- Ask students to identify the shape. If students have not worked with geometric shapes, offer choices such as square, triangle, rectangle, circle, and so forth. Draw the shape on the transparency sheet, allowing room to add a title for the map and a map legend/key. Then help students orient the shape on the overhead to the walls in the classroom.

  - Identify significant permanent structural features of the classroom such as doors, windows, closets, and bathrooms.
  - Introduce the map legend/key. Point out how difficult it is to label each element, but how easy it is to use shapes and/or colors to identify specific elements and label them in the legend/key. Create a legend/key on the transparency.
  - Identify significant movable features such as desks, tables, and computers. Do not create too many items. This map will be used as an extension activity. Make sure the students' desks are large enough to label with student names or initials.

### Independent Practice

- Have students come to the overhead to identify their own desks on the classroom map. Write either their name or initials on the appropriate desk symbol. Note: Some students may need extra help or some clues to find their own desk's position on the map.

### Closure/Reflection

- Ask students to define a map. Have them compare the building block map of the classroom to the map on the overhead transparency.
- Ask students what other elements they might add to the overhead map of the classroom. Ask them how they would represent these elements in the map legend/key.

## Extension/Application Activity 1.1

### LEVEL: GRADES 1 AND 2

- Make copies of the overhead transparency classroom map for each student to use. This might be a "seatwork" activity that follows up the next day, or a project at a classroom center.

  - Have students add more elements to the map. The number depends on the class and the curricular needs.
  - Have students include a symbol and label in the legend/key to identify each element added to the basic map.

**Figure 1.1** Jan's first-grade students' map lesson Extension 1.1.

## *Extension/Application Activity 1.2*

### LEVEL: GRADES 1 AND 2 (GRADE 3 IF THE EXPECTATIONS ARE INCREASED)

Allow students to apply what they have learned about creating maps with this follow-up experience. This may be a separate lesson, a morning work assignment, or a project at a classroom center.

- Discuss students' favorite part of the school playground. Ask what they would include if they were in charge of building a new school playground.
- Model how to create a map of the playground as it currently exists. (Sometimes students feel compelled to reproduce the teacher's creative choices, so modeling the existing playground eliminates that possibility.) Be sure to include a legend/key to identify the elements in the map. Discuss or model how color coding might be useful.

  - Provide sheets of 12 × 18-inch manila paper or newsprint.
  - Demonstrate how to use a fold to create a line between the legend/key and the map (approximately one-third for the legend and two-third for the playground map).
  - Encourage students to create a map of their own playground plan or allow them to create a map of the existing school playground. Both experiences require them to create a drawing of a mental map.

The following lesson was used with both first- and third-grade students. It was an introductory lesson for first grade and a review lesson for third. In the first grade, the teacher drew the two circles for the Venn diagram on a large sheet of butcher paper. The students provided information about maps and globes and directed the teacher to the correct portion of the Venn diagram where she wrote, rather than using the 3 × 5-inch cards used in the following lesson.

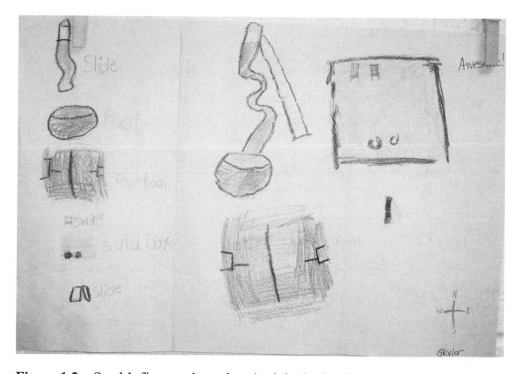

**Figure 1.2**   Sarah's first-grade students' original school playground map. Sarah used Extension 1.2 as a center project the week after the lesson.

## *Lesson Plan 1.2—Comparing Maps and Globes*

LEVEL: INTRODUCTORY FOR KINDERGARTEN AND GRADE 1; REVIEW FOR GRADES 2 AND 3

### Learning Goals

- Students will identify the characteristics of maps and globes.
- Students will compare and contrast the characteristics of maps and globes.
- Students will identify water and land on a globe.

### Assessment

- Informal assessment: Observation of discussion and position of cards in the Venn diagram.
- Potential formal assessment: Have each student compare and contrast characteristics of globes and maps in written form using the Venn diagram.
- Informal assessment: Anecdotal notes as each student identifies land and water on globe toss game in Extension Activity 1.3.

### Materials

- *Mapping Penny's World* (Leedy, 2000)
- World atlas or world map
- State map
- Inflatable globe
- Globe on stand
- Yarn—36 inches each of blue and green yarn with ends tied to create two circles
- 3 × 5-inch cards; at least one blank card for every two students and one labeled Globes, the other Maps

### Key Questions and/or Vocabulary

- Map: a drawing that shows what places look like from above and where they are located.
- Globe: spherical representation of the earth.
- Sphere: three-dimensional shape, ball.
- Atlas: a collection of maps.

### Procedure

#### *Motivation and Explanation*

- Ask students to describe how their parents decide to drive from one city or town to another. If they do not mention maps, show them the state map. Define *map* with the students if necessary. Ask what it is and what it shows. If students identify Mapquest (www.mapquest.com), explain that it is an online atlas that has many maps available for use.
- Tell students they are going to hear a book that features different kinds of maps. Read *Mapping Penny's World* (Leedy, 2000), showing the illustrations. Make the

read-aloud interactive by asking questions to guide thinking and accepting comments and questions as time allows.
- Show the students the globe on a stand. Ask what it is and what it shows.
- Define *globe* and *sphere*.

### Demonstration and Modeling

- Tell the students there are several things globes and maps have that are alike and several things that make them different. For example, maps and globes both have land and water identified on them. Globes show all of Earth, but not all maps do.
- Ask the students to describe a Venn diagram. Tell them you are going to use the two yarn circles to create a Venn diagram on the floor. Identify one circle with the Globes card and the other circle with the Maps card. Be sure to note that the intersection of the circles is for facts that are true of both maps and globes.
- Write the facts identified on three 3 × 5-inch cards:

  1. Maps and globes both have land and water on them.
  2. Globes always show all of Earth.
  3. Maps can show just one part of Earth.

- Read your cards and place them on the floor in the appropriate positions. Explain why they are placed that way.

### Guided Practice

- Ask students to provide another fact that you can write on a card. Write the fact on the card and then ask where the card should be placed on the Venn diagram. Confirm the validity of the fact and its placement with all students.

### Independent Practice

- Give each student or each pair of students a 3 × 5-inch card.
- Tell the students that they will now work in teams to provide a fact that tells about maps only, globes only, or that is true of both maps and globes.
- Guide students' thinking to make sure everyone can participate, particularly if they are struggling.
- Ask students to read their cards aloud and then place them on the Venn diagram.

### Closure/Reflection

- Look at all of the cards again as a class. Read them aloud as you pick them up from the Venn diagram. Ask students what facts they think were left out; have extra cards available on which to write these facts. Make sure to add facts that students should know and that were not included in the preceding activity.
- Tell the students the cards are being saved so that facts can be added as they continue to learn about maps and globes. Create a bulletin board using students' cards, or reproduce the content on a Venn diagram handout that students can keep as a review. If this is the case, be sure to return to it with additional facts as they are discussed in class.

## *Extension/Application Activity 1.3*

### LEVEL: KINDERGARTEN AND GRADE 1

- Have students form a circle in the classroom. Tell students that the class is going to play a game using the inflated globe, a game they could not play with a map.
- Discuss the differences that make this possible—the globe is spherical and map is flat. Note, however, that a map can be folded and easily transported, but it is more difficult to transport a globe.
- Rotate the globe, asking students to tell what they see on it. Accept appropriate answers and lead students to note that the globe has land and water.
- Ask students if there is more land or more water on the globe (and on Earth). If they do not know, tell them that the earth is about three-fourths water (oceans) and one-fourth land (continents). The game should help prove this fact.
- Set the rules for the Globe Toss game:

  - Call the name of the person to whom you are throwing the globe.
  - Gently toss the globe underhand.
  - Look to see where the student's right thumb is resting when the globe is caught; identify whether it is on water or land.

- Keep a tally as the game is played. Facilitate any problems. Play until each student has caught the globe once. Note: Occasionally it does turn out that you have more land than water tallies. If time permits, play until the point about more water is made.

Chris's third-grade students are responsible for knowing about imaginary lines that humans use to find locations and for being able to discuss them. Students must be able to identify the equator and prime meridian, as well as the four hemispheres: northern, southern, eastern, and western. Gail Gibbons's (1995) wonderful book *Planet Earth/ Inside Out* was used, but you might want to use another informational book to introduce these terms.

## Lesson Plan 1.3—Imaginary Lines

### LEVEL: INTRODUCTORY GRADE 2; REVIEW GRADES 3 AND 4

### Learning Goals

- Students will identify imaginary lines found on geographic representations.
- Students will identify the four hemispheres on the globe.

### Assessment

- Informal assessment: Observation of discussion.
- Informal assessment: Anecdotal notes as each child identifies hemispheres during globe toss game.

### Materials

- *Planet Earth/Inside Out* (Gibbons, 1995)
- Inflatable globe with yarn taped along the equator and prime meridian (See Figure 1.3)

### Key Questions and/or Vocabulary

- Why do humans use imaginary lines?
- Equator
- Hemispheres

### Procedure

#### Motivation and Explanation

- Gather students in a comfortable place to read the book. Ask them what they know about Earth. Accept multiple answers.
- Tell students to think about the imaginary lines that humans use when they talk about different parts of Earth. Encourage them to look for the names of these lines as you read.
- Make the read-aloud interactive by asking questions to guide thinking and accepting comments and questions as time allows. After you complete the reading, ask students for the names of the imaginary lines. Discuss where they are located. Use terms like around the "bulge" in the center of the earth and "through the poles."

#### Demonstration and Modeling

   Hold up the globe on which you have taped yarn over the equator and the prime meridian. Review the term *sphere*. Ask students what they think hemisphere means. You may need to provide the clue that *hemi* means half.

- Demonstrate that the equator divides the earth into the northern and southern hemispheres. Everything north–between the equator and the North Pole is in the northern hemisphere. Avoid saying "above the equator." Everything between the equator and the South Pole is in the southern hemisphere. Avoid saying "below the equator."

**Figure 1.3**   This inflatable globe has yarn attached to identify the equator and prime meridian.

- Demonstrate that the prime meridian divides the earth into the eastern and western hemispheres. Be sure to point out that this imaginary line passes through the two poles. Two clues to help students distinguish between eastern and western hemisphere are (1) North America is in the western hemisphere and (2) Asia, the largest continent, and Australia, a continent and a country, are in the eastern hemisphere.

### Guided Practice

- Have students form a circle to play a game using the inflated globe.
- Set the rules for this Globe Toss game:

  - Call the name of the person to whom you are throwing the globe.
  - Gently toss the globe underhand.
  - Look to see where the student's right thumb is resting when the globe is caught; identify which hemisphere it is in. Note: Each location can have two correct

answers. For example, a thumb on Greenland is in the western and northern hemi-spheres.

- Toss the globe, identifying the hemispheres until every student has had a turn.
- Check the world map in the classroom for the imaginary lines. Compare them to the globe.

### Closure/Reflection

- Ask students why humans use imaginary lines.
- Define and locate the equator; prime meridian; and eastern, western, northern, and southern hemispheres.
- Ask students to identify the hemisphere in which (name several countries or oceans) is located. Allow students to use the world map or the globe to help answer the question.

## Extension/Application Activity 1.4

LEVEL: GRADES 2, 3, AND 4 (DEPENDS ON TYPE OF MAP AND DIFFICULTY OF CLUES)

This can be an entire lesson or an application of the imaginary lines lesson.

- Prepare a map with a number and letter grid
- Prepare 3 × 5-inch cards containing clues about locations of cities or landmarks on the map.
- Demonstrate how to use the numbers and letters to locate a specific spot.
- Hand out clues to student pairs and allow them to find the answers. Share with the whole group.
- Use this map and grid as a center where students practice finding the clues you create, or have them create clues for their peers.

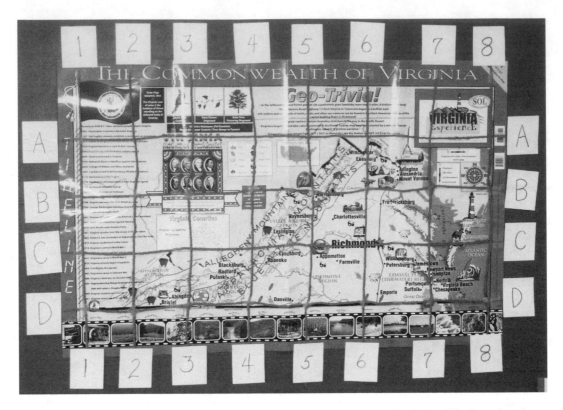

**Figure 1.4** A yarn grid over a map of Virginia helps students find specific locations.

## *Lesson Plan 1.4—Using Cardinal Directions*

### LEVEL: GRADES 1 AND 2 (REVIEW)

### Learning Goals

- Students will identify the four cardinal directions: north, south, east, west.
- Students will use cardinal directions to locate specific places on a map.

### Assessment

- Informal assessment: Observation during discussion and during the small group map activity.
- Potential formal assessment: Extension Activity 1.5.

### Materials

- Variety of maps and globes
- Small floor maps: identify with name or number/letter. These can sometimes be found in a dollar store, or create your own using a plastic tablecloth intended for a boy's birthday party (See Figure 1.5). Cut the tablecloth where the road pattern repeats. Create your own compass rose and attach it to a corner of the map.
- Small cars
- 3 × 5-inch cards with directions (5–6 for each specific floor map) placed in a small plastic bag for organization
  Example:

  1. Start at the compass rose.
  2. Go north to the circle.
  3. Go around the circle to the parking lot.
  4. Where are you? eciffo tsop

(Note: the answer is spelled backward at the end—here it is the post office.)

### Key Questions and/or Vocabulary

- Cardinal directions
- Compass rose
- North, south, east, west

### Procedure

#### *Motivation and Explanation*

- Pull down the classroom map of the world or the United States, lay out various maps, and provide a globe on a stand and the inflated globe for students to examine. Ask them to decide, with a partner, how they would explain to a friend how to go from one location to another on any of these items.
- Solicit responses after two minutes. Accept responses and ask for clarification if necessary.

- Reinforce the terms, directions, compass rose, or any of the four cardinal directions.
- If students have not used these terms, introduce and define the terms and their uses.

### Demonstration and Modeling

- Gather students on the floor around a small plastic map.
- Encourage students to identify the elements found on the map.
- Point out the compass rose—if they do not identify it—and ask them to explain how it would be used on this map.
- Hand one of the cards to a student, and ask the student to read the directions slowly as you demonstrate how to move the car along the map. Engage in some think-aloud strategies to help students think about using the compass rose and cardinal directions to facilitate the journey.

### Guided Practice

- Allow one student to manipulate the car while another student reads another card. Ask the student to explain his/her movements.
- Make sure all students understand the use of the compass rose.

### Independent Practice

- Divide students into small groups of four.
- Set behavioral expectations:

  - Everyone should have a turn with the car and reading a card for another student.
  - No one may stand or sit on the map.

- Circulate to support their actions and to informally assess their ability to use the compass rose and cardinal directions to get to the specific locations on the cards as students engage in this independent activity.
- Have each group create a directions card for the teacher to use to move from one place to another.

### Closure/Reflection

- Discuss students' experiences. Have them read some of their direction cards.
- Ask students to define compass rose, cardinal directions, and where the four cardinal directions are located in relation to each other. For example: "If north is on the left, where will south be?"

**Figure 1.5**   Students work independently using direction cards, cars, and a floor map.

## *Extension/Application Activity 1.5*

### LEVEL: GRADES 1, 2, AND 3 (DEPENDS ON TEACHER'S EXPECTATIONS)

This activity engages students in the use of prepositions to describe where they are in space. The ability to use prepositions is a natural way to prepare students to use relative locational terms such as *south of* when examining or drawing a map. This activity can be set as morning work or a project in a center.

- Use a digital camera to take a series of staged photos of students in your classroom. Place the students in various positions that demonstrate a preposition (See Figure 1.6).
- Transfer the pictures to your computer. Import thumbnail-size copies of the photos into the top of a word document. At the bottom of the document list the prepositions that can be used to describe students' positions in the photos.

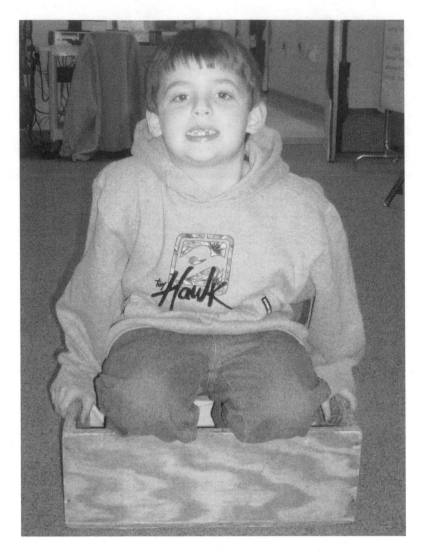

**Figure 1.6** Here Jordan poses in a box for a photo. Sarah's first graders used the photo as a prompt to write their sentences with prepositions describing relative positions in space. "Jordan is *in* the box." (Extension Activity 1.5)

• Have students cut out each photo and glue it onto a piece of storybook or notebook paper. Next to each photo students should write a complete sentence about the photo using one of the prepositions (which may be glued into the sentence or written and underlined).

## *Extension/Application Activity 1.6*

### LEVEL: GRADES 1, 2, 3, AND 4

Allow students to apply their knowledge of a compass rose and the cardinal directions using this activity. It may be set as a morning work activity or a project in a center.

• Use a commercially produced map or create one. Make sure it has a compass rose and map legend/key.

**Figure 1.7**   Sarah used Extension Activity 1.5 as a morning assignment in her first-grade students' morning journals. They copied the map into their journals and then wrote directions described on the board, using cardinal directions. Sarah and the class discussed the possible answers to the three questions when everyone had finished.

- List several sets of directions that use the cardinal directions. Ask students to write the ending point of each set of directions.
- Have students create several sets of directions. These may be student-selected, or teacher-selected, based on grade level.

## Review Game—"I Have . . .Who Has?"

### LEVEL: GRADES 1 AND 2 (WITH VISUAL INFORMATION) GRADES 3 AND 4 (WORDS ALONE)

"I have . . .Who has?" is a great way to facilitate listening as students review vocabulary. Since Sarah's students are first graders and benefit from visual as well as written information, her game cards often have a visual aspect to reinforce the concepts. Words alone can also be used.

### *Preparation*

- Use 3 × 5-inch cards for words alone. Use larger cards to include visual elements.
- Create a list of vocabulary and their definitions.

For example:

cardinal directions: north, south, east, west

map: a drawing that shows places from above and where they are located

land: the land masses on the globe are usually colored green

globe: a round model of the earth

- Write the first definition at the top of the card following the words "I have." Note: In Sarah's method, the definition uses a picture (See top card in Figure 1.8). Using words alone it would say, "I have north, south, east, west."
- Write the first vocabulary word at the bottom of the card using the phrase, "Who has." Note: In both methods, the phrase becomes a full sentence, e.g., "Who has land?"
- Continue in this manner so that the cards contain a chain of questions with the vocabulary word at the bottom of the card and the definition on the top of the next card. The last card's question should be answered by a definition placed at the top of the first card.
- Another way to prepare these cards is to place the "Who has" portion of the phrase on one side of an index card and the "I have" portion on the back side of an index card using the same order and logic as above. This works best with older students, because they have to pay attention to both sides of the card. If you use the label command in your Tools menu, create the phrases on labels and attach them to index cards. Laminate the cards, if possible.

**Figure 1.8** Consecutive cards for primary students to play "I have…Who has?" as a review activity.

### *Play*

- Each student should have one card. If there are more vocabulary cards than students, give a second card to students you believe can handle two.
- Begin with any card as the cards should be continuously linked. Be sure to read the question at the bottom.
- Read them through two times; more if necessary.

Sarah creates a great competition by timing the first read through the cards. She posts the time on the board and challenges the students to beat their time. After they have successfully moved through the cards two or three more times, she has her students trade the cards and try again. She uses the cards several days before the final assessment so that students have played with several different cards and have listened through the vocabulary list with definitions numerous times.

# Setting the Stage

In addition to having the text sets available for students' use, consider other ways to prepare the classroom environment. For example:

- Create engaging teaching and interactive bulletin boards.
- Place age-appropriate map puzzles at centers for students to assemble.
- Hang posters and maps around the room.
- Suspend inflatable globes from the ceiling.

## *A Unique Idea*

Figure 1.9 shows a unique interactive teaching tool hanging in the hallway outside the school office at the A. C. Moore Elementary School in Columbia, South Carolina. Three first-grade teachers, Tonia Griffin, Mary Brown, and Emily Carpenter, had a vision for improving students' social studies scores on the state assessment test. The three proposed an Inquiry Research Project titled, "Meet the World at A. C. Moore." A huge mural of the continents of the world was mounted on the wall. Funding came from a Teacher Quality Enhancement Partnership Grant with the University of South Carolina,

**Figure 1.9** This mural at A. C. Moore Elementary School in Columbia, South Carolina is an interactive teaching tool. The individual land masses were created to scale on plywood and painted by artist Carl Copeland, then mounted on a wall in the main hallway.

facilitated by Dr. Jane Zenger, the USC Faculty Consultant. Grant monies were also used to purchase books and media for the whole school, which are housed in the library.

Artist Carl Copeland created the continents to scale on plywood. He then painted them and they were mounted on the wall. The first phase of the project added animals from each continent. Other symbols, music, art, and landmarks from every continent will be added over time. The international students at A. C. Moore Elementary School were each invited to fill out a personal information sheet about their heritage. Each was mounted on the wall with a photo next to the continent of their native country.

A local television station that has a regular feature, "This Day in History," visited the school to film an interview with Amelia Earhart performed by fifth-grade students. Amelia, who had just completed her historic trip across the Atlantic, had marked her route on the interactive mural. It is too soon to know whether the mural has positively impacted the social studies scores, but the ripples are being felt as other teachers in the building have identified how they can use the interactive mural to support their curriculum.

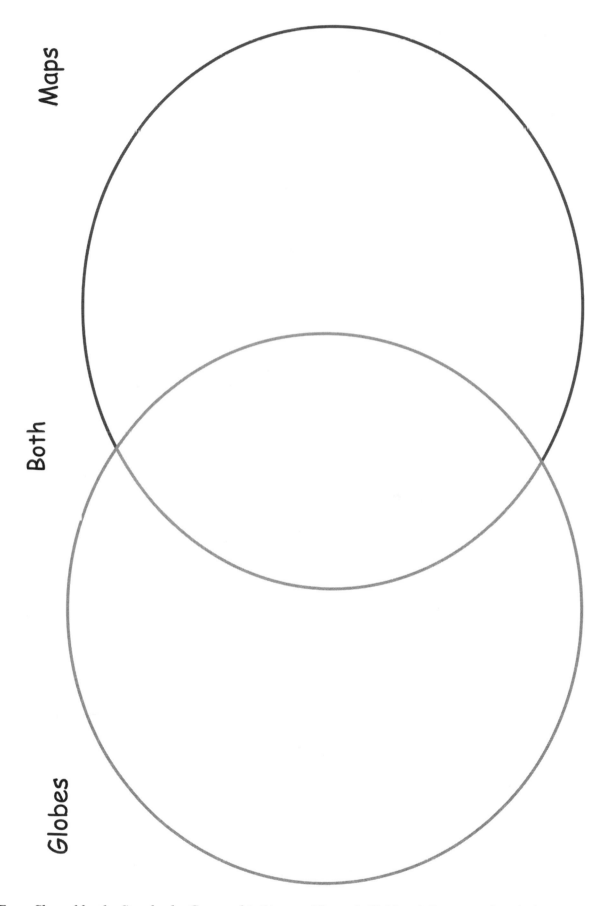

Maps

Both

Globes

From *Shaped by the Standards: Geographic Literacy Through Children's Literature* by Linda K. Rogers. Westport, CT: Teacher Ideas Press/Libraries Unlimited. Copyright © 2008.

## CHAPTER 2

# Places and Regions

Physical and human phenomena are spatially distributed over Earth's surface. The outcome of *Geography for Life* is a geographically informed person (1) who sees meaning in the arrangement of things in space; (2) who sees relations between people, places, and environments; (3) who uses geographic skills; and (4) who applies spatial and ecological perspectives to life situations.

## PLACES AND REGIONS

The identities and lives of individuals and peoples are rooted in particular places and in those human constructs called regions.

The geographically informed person knows and understands:

4. The physical and human characteristics of places.
   a. The physical characteristics of places (e.g., landforms, bodies of water, soil, vegetation, and weather and climate).
   b. The human characteristic of places (e.g., population distributions, settlement patterns, languages, ethnicity, nationality, and religious beliefs).
   c. How physical and human processes together shape places.

5. That people create regions to interpret Earth's complexity.
   a. The concept of region as an area of Earth's surface with unifying geographic characteristics.
   b. The similarities and differences among regions.
   c. The ways in which regions change.

6. How culture and experience influence people's perceptions of places and regions.
   a. How to describe the student's own community and region from different perspectives.
   b. Ways in which different people perceive places and regions.

*Geography for Life: National Geography Standards* (National Council for the Social Studies, 1994, pp. 34, 113–117).

The performance expectations for Places and Regions involve the themes of Place and Region. Place is the physical and human characteristics of a given location. Identifying the physical location of the story is actually discussing the setting. Students often engage in this activity during reading instruction. These concepts are not as difficult for students to understand as regional determinations.

Regions are a human construct. A region is an area that displays unity in terms of selected criteria. Regions of the United States, usually determined by location, are taught in most fourth grades. Home state studies are included in third- or fourth-grade curriculums. Regions can also be determined by a particular characteristic such as landforms, governmental unit, ethnicity, or religion. In early grades, students often study regions organized by landform or climate.

## Text Sets—Tour the USA, Tasting Places in the USA, Same and Different Around the World

### Tour the USA

The first two text sets relate to the most typical study found in elementary classrooms: regions of the United States and home state studies. The first set, Tour the USA, is a collection of books that look at the country as a whole by examining specific locales. Within this set are two types of books. One set contains books that look at the country more affectively; they tap into our emotions about this huge country—nostalgia, patriotism, pride, joy, and amazement. The authors and illustrators are selective in the locales they include in the book. They justify their choices and the reader is drawn into their visions of the United States.

Katherine Lee Bates's words in *America the Beautiful* served as inspiration for three uniquely illustrated books found in this set. Another excellent book in this collection is Kathy Jakobsen's interpretation of Woody Guthrie's famous *This Land Is Your Land*. *Across America, I Love You* is a unique blend of parental and patriotic love. Rylant's *Tulip Sees America* has a whimsical, yet reverent, feel to it, and Scillian's *A Is for America* is a lovely mix of lyric and informational text that is consistent in the Sleeping Bear Press's alphabet books.

Do not miss out on Diane Siebert's *Tour America: A Journey Through Poems and Art*. It may be a bit sophisticated for younger students, but the rhythm of her verse is a great "listen" and the art is truly spectacular.

Any of the books in this first set can be a used as a model for student writing and illustrating. What a wonderful way to integrate information and emotion.

The other type of books in this text set is informational books that have a variety of approaches to presenting data. In combination they provide a rich resource for that state report every student completes at some point in school. None of these books lend themselves to the typical read-aloud experience, but they model different ways to present factual information about regions and states. Hopkin's collection of poetry that is organized by regions and accompanied by state facts is an interesting cross between the affective and informational approach.

### Tour the USA

#### Aesthetic

- Bates, Katherine Lee. (1993). *America the Beautiful*. New York: Antheneum Books for Young Readers.

- Bates, Katherine Lee. (2003). *America the Beautiful.* New York: G. P. Putnam's Sons.
- Bates, Katherine Lee. (2004). *America the Beautiful.* New York: Little, Brown and Company.
- Guthrie, Woody. (1998). *This Land Is Your Land.* Boston: Little, Brown and Company.
- Hopkins, Lee Bennett. (2000). *My America: A Poetry Atlas of the United States.* New York: Scholastic, Inc.
- Loomis, Christine. (2000). *Across America, I Love You.* New York: Hyperion Books for Children.
- Rylant, Cynthia. (1998). *Tulip Sees America.* New York: The Blue Sky Press.
- Scillian, Devin. (2001). *A Is for America.* Chelsea, MI: Sleeping Bear Press.
- Siebert, Diane. (2006). *Tour America: A Journey Through Poems and Art.* San Francisco: Chronicle Books.

### *Informational*

- Blanton, Lynne & Hedberg, Betsy. (2003). *States.* Lincolnwood, IL: Publications International, Ltd.
- Buller, Jon, Schade, Susan, Cocca-Leffler, Maryann, Holub, Joan, Kelley, True, & Regan, Dana. (2003). *Smart about the Fifty States: A Class Report.* New York: Scholastic.
- Cheney, Lynne. (2006). *Our 50 States: A Family Adventure across America.* New York: Simon and Schuster Books for Young Readers.
- Davis, Kenneth C. (2001). *Don't Know Much about the 50 States.* New York: Scholastic, Inc.
- Krull, Kathleen. (1997). *Wish You Were Here: Emily's Guide to the 50 States.* New York: A Doubleday Book for Young Readers.
- Leedy, Loreen. (1999). *Celebrate the 50 States.* New York: Holiday House.
- Sis, Peter. (2004). *The Train of States.* New York: Greenwillow Books.

## *Tasting Places in the USA*

The second text set, Tasting Places in the USA, is a mix of books that represent specific places in the United States. They share the physical and human characteristics or "place" of specific locales. These are the types of books that support instruction for a home-state unit or patriotic symbols. Look for books specific to your state's physical and human characteristics.

*The Scrambled States of America,* a clever fantasy, sets the stage for students to think about the impact of location on the characteristics of place. *Liberty's Journey* is a fantasy journey with the Statue of Liberty across the United States, and *Looking at Liberty* examines the story of how the statue became a symbol of New York City and freedom. Cherry's curious armadillo, Sasparillo, tours Texas, and Munro's readers examine Texas from inside and out. *A River Ran Wild* is set in New England and traces the life of the Nashua River Valley over 500 years. The others in the set represent the new type of alphabet book that is content-rich and teaches as it entertains.

### Tasting Places in the USA

- Cherry, Lynne. (1992). *A River Ran Wild.* San Diego: A Gulliver Green Book.
- Cherry, Lynne. (1994). *The Armadillo from Amarillo.* San Diego: A Gulliver Green Book.
- DiPucchio, Kelly. (2004). *Liberty's Journey.* New York: Hyperion Books for Children.
- Keller, Laurie. (1998). *The Scrambled States of America.* New York: Scholastic, Inc.
- Munro, Roxie. (2001). *The Inside-Outside Book of Texas.* New York: Sea Star Book.
- Stevenson, Harvey. (2005). *Looking at Liberty.* NY: HarperCollins Publisher.

### *Alphabet Books*

- Kane, Kristen. (2003). *K Is for Keystone: A Pennsylvania Alphabet.* Chelsea, MI: Sleeping Bear Press.
- Melmed, Laura. Krauss. (2003). *Capital!: Washington D.C. from A to Z.* NY: HarperCollins Publishers.
- Noble, Trisha Hakes. (2005). *One for All: A Pennsylvania Number Book.* Chelsea, MI: Sleeping Bear Press.
- Schonberg, Marcia. (2000). *B Is for Buckeye.* Chelsea, MI: Sleeping Bear Press.
- Zschock, Martha, and Zschock, Heather. (2002). *Journey Around New York from A to Z.* Beverly, MA: Commonwealth Editions.

## *Same and Different Around the World*

"The identities and lives of individuals and peoples are rooted in particular places and in those human constructs called regions" (*Geography for Life,* p. 34). At a time when diversity issues come to the forefront of our lives, we tend to treat differences as negatives and ignore similarities. In the following text set, Same and Different Around the World, the books encourage readers to celebrate the differences and acknowledge similarities. Cave and Kinkade provide photographic evidence of same and different, while Montanari's and Vyner's books use illustrations to support the text.

Within the text set is a subset, Africa, which looks at the characteristics of place in several African locales. The children's activities in these books have common elements, yet are specific to place. Africa is a huge continent that should not be defined by one culture, as Musgrove's classic *Ahanti to Zulu* demonstrates. Yet, Onyefulu points out that there is commonality in life in Nigeria and other places in Africa.

### Same and Different Around the World

### *General*

- Cave, Kathryn. (1998). *W Is for World: A Round-The-World ABC.* London, Great Britain: Frances Lincoln Children's Books.
- Eduar, Gilles. (2002). Gigi and Zachary's Around-the-World-Adventure: A Seek-and-Find Game. San Francisco: Chronicle Books LLC.
- Hamanaka, Sheila. (1994). *All the Colors of the Earth.* New York: Scholastic, Inc.

- Katz, Karen. (1999). *The Colors of Us*. New York: Scholastic, Inc.
- Kinkade, Sheila. (2006). *My Family*. Watertown, MA: Charlesbridge.
- Montanari, Donata. (2001). *Children Around the World*. Toronto, ON: Kids Can Press Ltd.
- Pinkney, Sandra L. (2000). *Shades of Black: A Celebration of Our Children*. New York: Scholastic, Inc.
- Vyner, Tim. (2001). *World Team*. Brookfield, CT: Roaring Brook Press.

## *Africa*

- Aardema, Verna. (1992). *Bringing the Rain to Kapiti Plain*. New York: Puffin Books.
- Bulion, Leslie. (2002). *Fatuma's New Cloth*. North Kingstown, RI: Moon Mountain Publishing.
- McDonald, Suse. (1995). *Nanta's Lion*. New York: Morrow Junior Books.
- Mollel, Tolowa M. (1999). *My Rows and Piles of Coins*. New York: Clarion Books.
- Musgrove, Margaret. (1992). *Ashanti to Zulu*. NY: Puffin Books.
- Olaleye, Isaac. (2001). *Bikes for Rent!* New York: Orchard Books.
- Onyefulu, Ifeoma. (1996). *OGBO: Sharing Life in an African Village*. New York: Gulliver.
- Onyefulu, Ifeoma. (1997). *A Is for Africa*. New York: A Puffin Unicorn.

The Asia text set demonstrates the way culture and experience influence people's perceptions of places and regions. Chin-Lee's alphabet book, *A Is for Asia*, celebrates the diversity in the world's largest continent. In *Good-bye, 382 Shin Dang Dong* and *The Trip Back Home*, young girls experience the challenges of living in two distinctly different countries and cultures (Korea and the United States). Seven-year-old Mimiko takes the reader on a tour of her favorite places in *I Live in Tokyo*. Allen Say's *Kamishibai Man* returns to the city where he worked as a young man and is surprised by the physical changes but delighted by the same human reaction to his gift of storytelling. Say's other book, *Tea with Milk*, perhaps a bit sophisticated for younger students, is a charming story about a girl and her parents who view the two countries in which they live, the United States and Japan, very differently. Yin's two books tell the stories of three Chinese brothers who meet the challenges of immigration in mid-1800 America.

## Asia

- Chin-Lee, Cynthia. (1997). *A Is for Asia*. New York: Orchard Books.
- Park, Frances and Park, Ginger. (2002). *Good-bye, 382 Shin Dang Dong*. Washington, D.C.: National Geographic Society.
- Say, Allen. (1999). *Tea with Milk*. Boston: Houghton Mifflin Company.
- Say, Allen. (2005). *Kamishibai Man*. Boston: Houghton Mifflin Company.
- Takabayaski, Mari. (2001). *I Live in Tokyo*. Boston: Houghton Mifflin Company.
- Wong, Janet S. (2000). *The Trip Back Home*. San Diego: Harcourt, Inc.
- Yin. (2006). *Brothers*. New York: Philomel Books.
- Yin. (2000). *Coolies*. New York: Philomel Books.

## Teaching Ideas—Lesson Plans and Extension/Application Activities

Humans organize space by using regions. A particularly challenging concept for young children is that they can be in several political regions at the same time. Political regions, usually determined by governments, include city, county, school district, and so forth. This lesson uses Lynne Cherry's clever text to ask the question, "Where am I in space?" and Sasparillo, the Armadillo, resolves the issue more dramatically and concretely. But, the concept is transferable.

The *Armadillo from Amarillo* and reproducible pages were used with first graders. They listened to a tape of the story and then completed the concentric rectangles and map legend at a classroom listening center during the second week of the unit. The learning experience is provided here as a formal lesson rather than as a listening center activity.

## *Lesson Plan 2.1—Where Am I in Space?*

### LEVEL: INTRODUCTORY GRADES 1 AND 2; REVIEW GRADES 3

### Learning Goals

* Students will identify the political regions in which they are located.
* Students will place the political regions in order by size.

### Assessment

* Informal assessment: Observation of discussion during read-aloud and when examining the United States and world maps.
* Formal assessment: Concentric rectangle activity sheet.

### Materials

* *The Armadillo from Amarillo* by Lynne Cherry
* World map
* United States map
* *Armadillo Rectangles* worksheets
* *Armadillo Legends* worksheets
* 9 × 12-inch manila paper
* scissors
* glue
* crayons

### Key Questions and/or Vocabulary

* city: a place where a large number of people live close together
* state: a political community under one government
* country: a nation or its territory
* continent: a large mass of land surrounded by oceans
* planet: a celestial body orbiting a star

### Procedure

#### *Motivation and Explanation*

* Ask the students, "Where are we?" As they answer, for example, "in the classroom or school," say, "But I thought we were in" and name another of the political regions.
* Continue these questions until you can finally say, "So, do you think we can be in more than one place at once?" Students should conclude that the same place can be called many things, which is what you want them to discover.
* Tell students to listen carefully as *The Armadillo from Amarillo* is read to find out where the armadillo is. List the first four vocabulary words on the board. Tell students to listen for these words as well.
* Read the book and show the illustrations. Make the read-aloud interactive by asking questions to guide thinking and accepting comments and questions as time allows.

- Make notes next to the vocabulary words as you discuss them with students during the reading.

### Demonstration and Modeling

- Finish reading the book, and tell the students that you think you know where Sasparillo is in space. Say, "He's an armadillo, in the city of Amarillo, in the" Stop at this point and begin to draw a rectangle. Put a small drawing of an armadillo in the rectangle.
- Create a map legend/key that has four small squares next to the drawing. As you draw the rectangle and name it, color the rectangle and a box in the legend/key. Label the box "armadillo."

### Guided Practice

- Draw a larger rectangle around the rectangle with the armadillo and ask what it represents (Amarillo). Have the students help to label it in the legend/key.

### Independent Practice

- Distribute the activity sheets. Clarify the directions with the students and note the work done together.

**Figure. 2.1** A first-grader's completed activity sheet with legend.

### *Closure/Reflection*

- Discuss where Sasparillo was in space. As the students provide the information, have them draw it on the blackboard or on the overhead projector so that visual as well as verbal information is available. Ask students where they are in space. Use the same concentric rectangles, but start with a student (or yourself) and use the appropriate regions for your location. Be sure to lead students to understand that any one location can actually be defined or named by multiple names.
- Depending on the age and sophistication of the students, increase the number of regions to include such things as school districts, townships, and counties within the state and regions (northeast, etc.) within the United States.

## *Extension/Application Activity 2.1—Me on the Map*

### LEVEL: KINDERGARTEN (MUCH TEACHER SUPPORT), GRADES 1 AND 2

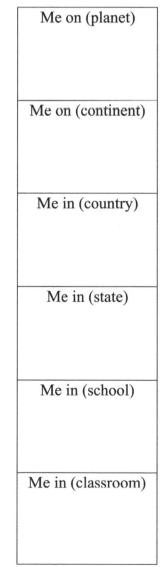

- Allow students to apply what they have learned about how one location can be identified in a variety of ways with this application activity. This may be a separate lesson or a project at a classroom listening center.
- Read the book, *Me on the Map* by Joan Sweeney, to the class or have it recorded so that students can listen at a center.
- Discuss the various places the girl describes as she tells where she is on the map.
- Determine, as a class, where they, as students, are located.
- Have students place themselves in six regions: planet, continent, country, state, school, and classroom. Or, eliminate planet and include city/town between state and school (See Figure 2.2). Allow several days for this activity if students complete only one illustration per day.
- Tape the pages together and hang them in the classroom.

When students engage in state studies, the curriculum includes an examination of the landform regions within the state. The following lesson was created by Lauren who taught it in a fourth-grade class. Lauren's students used teacher-made templates of the regions to trace each region from the textured papers they had created in the classroom the previous week. Directions for making textured papers and photo samples follow this lesson plan in Extension/Application Activity 2.2.

The fifth-grade students at Hyatt Park Elementary in Columbia, South Carolina, also created landform region maps. They used pieces of cardboard on which they drew the shape of their state and used different colors of modeling clay to depict the landform regions (See Figure 2.3).

**Figure 2.2** *Me on the Map* Extension diagram.

Although each final landform map looks different because of the materials used, each demonstrates student learning of the same concept. Select the product that meets the students' needs and works with available materials.

**Figure 2.3**    A Hyatt Park fifth-grade student's South Carolina map.

## *Lesson Plan 2.2—State Landform Regions*

### LEVEL: GRADE 4

### Learning Goals

- Students will identify, describe, and locate the landform regions of our state.
- Students will create a map depicting the landform regions of our state.

### Assessment

- Informal Assessment: Observation of discussion
- Formal Assessment: Landform region map with textured paper

    ✓+ map displays all five regions with textured paper and labels; well crafted; no misspellings

    ✓ map displays five regions with textured paper and labels; some misspellings

    ✓– map is missing one or more regions and/or labels; poorly crafted

### Materials

- *K Is for Keystone* by Kristen Kane
- Student-created textured paper (Extension/Activity 2.2)
- Blank map of Pennsylvania (one per student)
- Overhead transparency of Pennsylvania
- Pennsylvania region tracers (oaktag)—[Create several copies for each region to be shared in small groups]
- Glue
- Scissors

### Key Questions and/or Vocabulary

List the five regions on the blackboard

- Erie Plain: a low belt of sand and gravel where Lake Erie meets the land in northeastern PA
- Allegheny Plateau: covers the western and northern half of Pennsylvania; dominated by branching patterns of streams that cut into it; it is the most rugged landscape in Pennsylvania.
- Appalachian Ridge and Valley: distinctive belt of long, wooded ridges and broad agricultural valleys; this area is the foothills of the Allegheny range; there are valleys of rich farmland and others full of anthracite coal.
- Piedmont Plateau: a region of varied, hilly land; it is quite narrow in Pennsylvania; included in the piedmont plateau is Lancaster County, a fertile valley region that contains some of the best agricultural soils in the eastern United States.
- Coastal Plain: a low belt of sand and gravel where the sea meets the land; it consists of sediment eroded off the Appalachians; only a narrow coastal plain occurs in southeastern Pennsylvania; most in Philadelphia.

## Procedure

### *Motivation and Explanation*

- Ask students to describe the physical features of Pennsylvania. Briefly share *K Is for Keystone* with students. Read the verses for every letter, but only read the informational paragraphs on the pages that refer to Pennsylvania's physical features.
- Remind students of the textured papers they recently created by saying, "Today you will examine the landform regions of our state and use the textured paper to distinguish one region from another."

### *Demonstration and Modeling*

- Divide the students into small working groups.
- Place the blank Pennsylvania map on the overhead projector. Tell the students that there are five landform regions in Pennsylvania. Direct the students' attention to the five regions listed on the board.
- Trace a line on the overhead to separate the Erie Plain from the Allegheny Plateau using the tracer for the Erie Plain. Describe it for the students.

### *Guided Practice*

- Distribute the blank maps and the Erie Plain tracers. Have students use the tracer to identify the Erie Plain on their maps.
- Describe the Alleghany Plateau. Ask students where they believe it is located. Demonstrate with the tracer and distribute the tracers to each group.
- Proceed to describe and demonstrate the location of the final three regions as students create and label the landform regions on their maps.

### *Independent Practice*

- Display the textured papers created by the class. Have them sorted by color or color families.
- Tell students they will be using their knowledge of the five landform regions and their experience using the tracers to show the landform regions with the textured papers.
- Make certain each student uses the five tracers on five different pieces of textured paper, gluing the resulting shape onto the blank map students have been using.
- Caution students about accuracy in tracing and cutting and gluing onto the state base. Show a sample.
- Allow students to work independently and provide support where needed.

### *Closure/Reflection*

- Share the final landform region maps with one another. Identify the location, name, and description of each region.

Lauren's fourth-grade class created textured papers several days before the lesson on landform regions of Pennsylvania. The textured papers were gathered into one class set from which students selected five different patterns. The final results were striking (See Figure 2.4).

A beautiful way to identify the regions in your state is through the use of visually textured papers. Students can create the papers as a center project over several days, or set up several centers that use different techniques and they can create them all at one time. Practice in advance so that you can demonstrate each method.

## *Extension/Application Activity 2.2—Creating Textured Papers*

### LEVEL: KINDERGARTEN–GRADE 4 (SMALLER GROUPS AND MORE STRUCTURE FOR YOUNGER STUDENTS)

### *Materials*

- newspapers to cover surface/table
- 5–10 sheets of copy paper for each student
- 2–3 watercolor sets for each center
- spray bottle with water
- materials to create texture

  - brushes
  - toothbrushes
  - sponge pieces (1 and 2-inch squares or rectangles)
  - crayons
  - screening, rough sandpaper, netting

- containers for water
- paper towels

### *Procedure*

- Cover the surface of each center table with newspaper. Wet the watercolors with water so that the water can saturate the cake of color. Continue to add water throughout this experience as needed to keep the watercolors rich.
- Set up four or five centers using these directions (by Dr. Patricia Pinciotti):

  - Sponging

    2–3 watercolor sets
    sponge pieces
    containers of water
    Wet the sponge pieces, squeezing out excess water. Dip the sponge into the paint. Dip in one color at a time or consider dipping in two colors at once. Use the sponge to fill the page with visual texture. Make certain to fill the entire page leaving very few white areas. Make a pattern while pressing the sponge onto the paper.

  - Wet on Wet

    2–3 watercolor sets
    clean sponge or large clean brush
    containers of water
    Wet the paper with a large brush or sponge. Then drip, spatter, or draw lines of color onto the paper. You should see the paint moving on the page. Move the paper to manipulate the moving of the color.

**Figure 2.4** These two maps depicting Pennsylvania landform regions include the following five regions beginning in the northwest corner and moving across the state to the southeast corner: Erie Plain, Alleghany Ridge, Appalachian Ridge and Valley, Piedmont Plateau, and Atlantic Coastal Plain.

- Dry Brush

  2–3 watercolor sets
  brushes
  containers of water
  Load the brush with paint and then dab the brush onto a paper towel or sponge to release the water. Brush across the surface of the paper creating marks that show the brush's texture.

- Spatter

  2–3 watercolor sets
  paintbrushes
  toothbrushes
  containers of water
  Use a paintbrush or toothbrush loaded with wet color. Tap the handle of the brush with a pencil or shake the brush to create dots or blobs of color on the page. The toothbrush will create a very fine spatter effect. Make sure to cover the page with texture

- Resist

  2–3 watercolor sets
  brushes
  containers of water
  crayons
  rough sandpaper, screening or netting
  Place the paper over a textured surface (sandpaper, screening, or netting). Take a crayon and rub it over the surface of the paper to lift the texture. Use one or many crayons on a page, but make certain to fill the page with crayon textures. Then brush watercolors over the crayon textures. Use different colors to create a contrasting pattern.

- Move from center to center demonstrating each technique. Use a different color at each center so that students will think about making a wide range of colored textured papers. Allow students to make one or two sheets of textured paper at each center. As they complete a paper, the paper should be carefully placed on the floor away from traffic patterns to dry.
- Divide the students into small groups (as many as the number of centers). Position each group at a different center. Establish a rotating pattern.
- Time the students at each center based on whether everyone can work at once or if there are two sets of artists at each center stop.
- Circulate through the centers and make certain the watercolor cakes have enough water to keep the colors rich. Assist students who need help and keep students on task.
- Begin the clean up when everyone has made textured paper at each center. Clean-up is an essential step.

  - Rinse all art tools, sponges, and brushes with clean water, wiggling them to make sure all the paint is removed.

- Reshape brushes and allow them to dry before putting them away.
- Let the watercolors air-dry or press a paper towel on the strip to absorb extra water.

- Gather all the textured papers after they have dried. Sort them by color and save them to be used to create the landform regions.
- Save the unused textured papers and the scraps for future use.

Shawn Norris teaches physical education at Hyatt Park Elementary in Columbia, South Carolina. Shawn's inquiry project questioned whether students' social studies scores on the state assessment would improve if they were engaged in kinesthetic learning. He proposed creating a room-size map of South Carolina. Funding came from a Teacher Quality Enhancement Partnership Grant with the University of South Carolina and was facilitated by Dr. Jane Zenger, the USC Faculty Consultant.

The South Carolina map was created on a 20 × 30-foot piece of beige indoor/outdoor carpet by a local artist, Carl Copeland (See Figure 2.5). He established to scale the state borders, county boundaries, and interstate highways. The six geographic regions (Coastal, Inner Coastal Plains, Outer Coastal Plains, Sand Hill, Piedmont, and Blue Ridge zones) were subtly indicated with wording. Spaces outside the state border include a huge compass rose (See Figure 2.6), a distance scale, the state flag, and the state seal, and a map legend/key lists the county names alphabetically. The art teacher at Hyatt Hill has continued to add symbols to each county. Also identified is the county seat and at least one unique landmark or industry or product (See Figure 2.7). The county name is represented by a number found in the key.

The first year Shawn created a two-week unit that fit within his physical education curriculum for fifth grade. He then expanded the units to include third through-fifth-grade students during the second year. For example, fifth-grade students were studying the Civil War and how South Carolina was impacted. They had also discussed some geographic terms and knew the geographic regions within the state. Shawn used the map in the gym during the two weeks of instruction, then rolled it up for storage. Fortunately, the principal found an open space in the building to display the map; now there is a map room where the floor map is available for everyone to use. Just like a computer lab, the map's use is scheduled. Now other teachers bring their students to the map room to extend and enhance their lessons.

Hyatt Park Elementary might be the only school with a map room and a large map of the home state, but many schools have maps of the United States and home states painted on blacktopped areas outdoors. Consider how your school might enhance its state map with more than the location of the state capital. Perhaps it could be a project for older students in the district. Maps are concrete symbols of regional constructs; the larger and more interactive the map, the easier it will be for students to make connections to the abstract concepts it holds.

## Lesson Plan 2.3—Physically Exploring the State

### LEVEL: GRADES 3 AND 4

### Learning Goals

- Students will identify and use the key features of the map.
- Students will read the map using the symbols.
- Students will identify landform regions of South Carolina.

### Assessment

- Informal assessment: Discussion about symbols and features
- Informal assessment: County relay game

### Materials

- Floor map
- 3 × 5-inch cards with county names

### Key Questions and/or Vocabulary

- state border/lines
- county
- interstate highway
- adjoining states
- geographic regions/zones: Coastal, Inner Coastal Plains, Outer Coastal Plains, Sand Hill, Piedmont, and Blue Ridge

### Procedure

#### Motivation and Explanation

- Gather the students along the outer edge of the state—without shoes.
- Tell the students to look at the pictures/symbols on the map.
- Ask the students to provide the names of the geographic regions found in South Carolina. Move to each spot on the map where the regions/zones are indicated. Give students clues as needed.
- Allow students two minutes to walk around on the map to look for the symbols.

#### Demonstration and Modeling

- Explain the following to the students:

  - Black line: the state line or state border. Have the students identify the states and landform that form the border (Tennessee, Georgia, Atlantic Ocean, North Carolina)
  - Green lines: county borders. Note that the green lines appear to create puzzle pieces that fit together to create the state. These are the counties. South Carolina has 46 counties.
  - Red lines: interstate highways. Note that the red lines have numbers on them. Ask students what they think these represent. The interstate highways cross over the state borders into other states.

### Guided Practice

- Review the symbols: black, red, and green lines and the regions/zones.
- Ask students if they noticed the numbers in each county. Show them the map legend/key that identifies the county name.
- Give each student two cards. Each card has the name of a county on it. Tell students to find the number that corresponds to the county name and place the card in the county on the number. When they find the counties, they should sit down outside the state line.
- Provide clues about the region in which the county is found as the students search for the county's location.
- Congratulate students for finding all 46 counties once everyone is settled. Ask them to share the strategies they used to find the locations and to tell about the symbols/pictures found within one of the counties they located.

### Independent Practice

- Tell the students that they are going to play a team game with the cards.
  - Divide the class into three groups.
  - Have one group play with the cards and the others sit along the border and watch. Remind them they can learn from what the other teams do.
  - Distribute the cards to the group, and tell them you will time how quickly they identify the 46 counties.
  - Compare their times and briefly discuss the strategies they used after all three groups have had a chance to play.

**Figure 2.5** The South Carolina floor map identifies bordering states, county lines, and major highways.

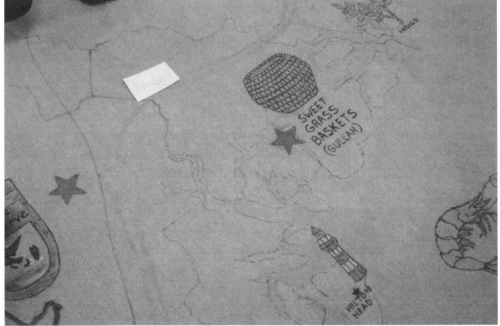

**Figures 2.6 and 2.7** A close look at a coastal county and the compass map rose and scale.

### *Closure/Reflection*

- Review what the students have learned by posing questions in a format found in standardized tests. For example, "Name the states that have a border with South Carolina. If I am in Columbia, what interstate highways would I use to get to the North Carolina border?" Have one student stand at the beginning point, one at the ending point, and have a third student move along the interstates to find the answer.

## Final Project—Report in a Can

Over the past decade of teaching, ideas have been gathered for final projects that allow students to show what they know in a variety of ways. "Report in a Can" is a unique format that can be used by young students and adapted for older students. Susan Gerken, a veteran second-grade teacher in Stroudsburg, Pennsylvania, developed this idea. She calls it "Story in a Can" and uses it in the spring of the year as a culminating experience for the Underground Unit.

The following lesson uses the basic format for Susan's strategy with the focus on state reports. The whole process requires a week or two, depending on the ability of the class, how much time is devoted to data collection in the classroom, and how the reports are used when completed.

### *Report in a Can*

#### LEVEL: GRADES 2 AND 3 (WITH MORE SUPPORT) GRADES 4

1. Tell students they will soon become state experts. Each student will learn as much as possible about one of the United States.
2. Determine how state selection will be made to avoid conflicts. It is unlikely that there are 50 students in the classroom, so limit the number of states to the number of students (plus one or two additional states for choice). Consider selecting a few states from each region of the United States. For example, *My America* by Hopkins organizes the states into eight regions, meaning that students can choose from three or four states from each region.
3. Ask the students to help generate a list of questions to be answered by their research. Be sure to have a list prepared to add to students' suggested questions. Consider the type of questions that will help students gain knowledge and understanding that match the state and national standards, and that stretch beyond the basic facts like capital, state flower, state bird, and the like. Determine the number of questions to include in this project. Consider identifying questions that *must* be answered and those that *can* be answered.
4. Create a data-gathering device once the list of questions is finalized. A variation on the Concept Square appears in Figure 2.8. This variation was prepared for several reasons.

   - Notice that the spaces are limited so that students need to take notes, not copy whole sentences, to help students avoid plagiarism.

- A one-page format (two sides) for each source is also provided because fourth graders should acknowledge the sources they use.

5. Model how to gather information. Select a state that has not been assigned to a student. Using a data-gathering device and one source, think aloud how to record the data, and then put the data into the appropriate square. An overhead projector or a piece of poster board that can be posted for students to refer to can be used (See Figure 2.8).

6. Collaborate with the school librarian on this project. Although classroom resources can be gathered, such as the ones listed in the Annotated Bibliography, the school library also has books that can be borrowed for your classroom or set aside for use in the library. One teacher schedules time with the librarian to assist small groups of students with their research. Allow students independence while also scaffolding their work according to their needs.

7. Transform the data into a report once collected. Present the report on 3 × 5-inch index cards that are held in a 13-oz. coffee can or similar size container.

   - Model the transformation. Read the first question and answer on your data gathering sheet. Write a complete sentence that answers the question using the information you wrote as the answer.

     For example: "Where is the state located?" Answer: "Middle Atlantic."
     Transformation: Pennsylvania is part of the Middle Atlantic States.
     This sentence should be written on the lined side of a 3 × 5-inch index card.

   - Model an illustration. An illustration or picture should appear on the unlined side of the index card. For the preceding transformed information, match the information with a drawing of the eastern portion of the United States and draw a colored arrow (to make it stand out) pointing to Pennsylvania.

   - Create a card for each source used in the report. Provide a format for referencing sources that students should use. By fourth grade, students are expected to include a reference list with a report. Consider using colored cards for the references.

8. Complete the Report in a Can. After all the data have been transformed into complete sentences and illustrations on index cards, create the cover for the report. Cut pieces of construction paper 5 1/2 × 13 inches. This becomes the cover that will wrap around the can.

   - Illustrate the cover appropriately. Be sure the cover includes the name of the state and the author. Remind students that ¾ inches on the right and left sides should be left blank because the sides will overlap when the cover is taped around the can. Explain to students that the cover invites the reader to open a book, so they want their cover to invite the reader to read their report.

   - Attach the cover by carefully lining it up on the can. Tape one end to the can using masking tape. Wrap the rest of the cover around the can and secure to the cover using transparent tape.

State Report Concept Squares

| STATE REPORT IN A CAN | |
|---|---|
| Information Source: <br> Title _____ <br><br> Date of Publication _____          Pages used _____ | |
| 1.  What is your state's name? | 2.  What is the capital? Where is it located? |
| 3.  Where is your state located? | 4.  How large is your state in area? How many people live in your state? |
| 5.  What is/are major industry(ies) in the state? | 6.  What is/are the major crop(s) in the state? |
| 7.  What major cities are found in the state? Why are they important? | 8.  What landforms/geographic characteristics are found in the state? |
| 9.  Why do people visit the state? | 10. etc. |

**Figure 2.8**   Use a table to create this modified concept squares format. It allows the teacher to place the questions students generate into the squares. Leave enough space for students to write notes that answer the questions. Use * to identify the "must-answer" questions.

9.   Follow-up Activities

- Place the state Reports in a Can in a special place in the classroom or library so that students can read each other's reports.
- Use the Reports in a Can to help students examine the information more closely. For example, sort the data cards by category. What data tell about geography? History? People? Places? Have students compare and contrast the information in these categories. Have a pair of students create a Venn diagram that formally compares and contrasts their states.
- Assign students to write a paragraph about one of the sorted categories to practice formal writing. Model the topic sentence and details based on your report or on a student's report data cards.

- Have the students carry their Reports in a Can to share with a younger student if you have younger "buddies" in the school.

One of the most appealing characteristics of the Report in a Can format is the acknowledgment that not every student will be able to find all of the answers to the all the questions. Thus every report is complete whether there are 8 completed data cards or 20. If you have carefully identified some required questions and left the rest as optional, or you have identified specific questions for particular groups of students, you make this a successful project for everyone. (Rogers, L. K. (2003). "A Report in a Can." *The Reading Teacher, 56*(8), 734–35.)

**The Armadillo from Amarillo Rectangles**

Color each rectangle. Put the rectangles together to show where Sasparilla was in space. Color the map legend to tell what each rectangle represents. Glue the rectangles and the map legend onto a piece of paper.

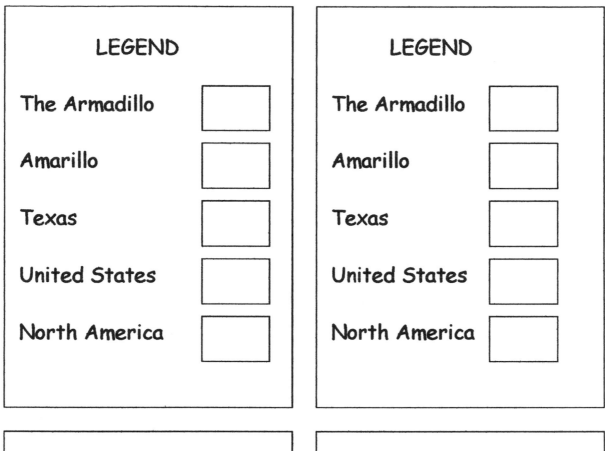

LEGEND

The Armadillo

Amarillo

Texas

United States

North America

LEGEND

The Armadillo

Amarillo

Texas

United States

North America

LEGEND

The Armadillo

Amarillo

Texas

United States

North America

LEGEND

The Armadillo

Amarillo

Texas

United States

North America

## CHAPTER 3

# Physical Systems

Physical and human phenomena are spatially distributed over Earth's surface. The outcome of *Geography for Life* is a geographically informed person (1) who sees meaning in the arrangement of things in space; (2) who sees relations between people, places, and environments; (3) who uses geographic skills; and (4) who applies spatial and ecological perspectives to life situations.

**PHYSICAL SYSTEMS**

Physical processes shape Earth's surface and interact with plant and animal life to create, sustain, and modify ecosystems.

The geographically informed person knows and understands:

7. The physical processes that shape the patterns of Earth's surface.
   a. The components of Earth's physical systems: the atmosphere, lithosphere (landforms), hydrosphere [e.g., oceans, lakes, rivers], and biosphere.
   b. How patterns (location, distribution, and association) of features on Earth's surface are shaped by physical processes [e.g., weather, wave action, freezing, thawing, gravity, soil-building].
   c. How Earth-Sun relations affect conditions on Earth.

8. The characteristics and spatial distribution of ecosystems on Earth's surface.
   a. The components of ecosystems.
   b. The distribution and patterns of ecosystems.
   c. How humans interact with ecosystems.

*Geography for Life: National Geography Standards* (National Council for the Social Studies, 1994, pp. 34, 118–121).

Science and social studies come together in geography standards 7 and 8. Students should be able to describe the components of Earth's physical systems and their impact on Earth, as well as plant and animal life. The study of ecosystems includes learning about the components of ecosystems, their distribution and pattern of distribution, and how humans interact with ecosystems. These standards reflect the themes of place and relationships within places.

# Text Sets—Earth's Systems, Ecosystems

This chapter provides two text sets. The first set, Earth's Systems, relates to landforms and the Earth/Sun relationship causing day and night, year, climate, seasons, and the water cycle. The Earth/Moon relationship causes tides and phases of the moon. The second text set, Ecosystems, looks at humans and/or animals and plants as they interact in a particular environment.

## *Earth's Systems*

Many of the books in Earth's Systems are nonfiction books. They provide clear explanations, photos, and diagrams to help the teacher and the student. Gibbon's informational *Planet Earth/Inside Out* and Keller's fantasy *Scrambled States of America* are perfect books for the beginning of a unit. Simon's classic *Sun* is full of beautiful photography and facts. Pipe's *Sun* is part of a student-friendly series of informational books. And Dyson's desire to send humans back to the moon provides an interesting narrative full of moon facts. Although this book is probably best used as a teacher resource, some fourth graders might enjoy her unique approach to teaching about the moon.

Bailey and Karas both deal with day and night and the year and seasons in a simple, yet substantive way. *Our Seasons* explains how seasons impact the weather, the natural world, and the human body. Seasons are also the focus in *Winter Is, Spring Song,* and *Winter Lullaby.* Banks informs the reader about how the hours of the day have special names used by the Gullah people on the barrier islands off the southeastern coast of the United States, and Bruchac reveals how Native Americans have kept track of the year by watching the 13 moons.

Children are impacted by extraordinary weather events in *One Lucky Girl, The Blizzard,* and *Sergio and the Hurricane.* Pairing books about the topic can spark your students' interest in the content of your unit. Waldman and Fourment present the water cycle in totally different, yet complementary formats. They are a perfect pairing. Your school librarian can help select book sets that include both nonfiction and fiction.

### Earth's Systems

#### *Nonfiction*

- Bailey, Jacqui. (2004). *Sun up, Sun down: The Story of Day and Night.* Minneapolis, MN: Picture Widow Books.
- Dyson, Marianne J. (2003). *Home on the Moon: Living on a Space Frontier.* Washington, D.C.: National Geographic Society.
- Fourment, Tiffany. (2004). *My Water Comes from the Mountains.* Lanham, MD: Roberts Rinehart Publishers.
- Gibbons, Gail. (1995). *Planet Earth/Inside Out.* New York: Morrow Junior Books.
- Karas, G. Brian. (2005). *On Earth.* New York: G. P. Putnam's Sons.
- Lin, Grace, and McKneally, Ranida T. (2006). *Our Seasons.* New York: Charlesbridge.

- Pipe, Jim. (2005). *Sun.* Mankato, MN: Stargazer Books.
- Schaefer, Lola M. (2006). *An Island Grows.* New York: Greenwillow Books.
- Simon, Seymour. (2003). *Earth: Our Planet in Space.* New York: Simon & Schuster Books for Young Readers.
- Waldman, Neil. (2003). *The Snowflake.* Brookfield, CT: The Millbrook Press.

### *Fiction*

- Banks, Sara H. (1997). *A Net to Catch Time.* New York: Alfred A. Knopf.
- Bruchac, Joseph and London, Jonathan. (1992). *Thirteen Moons on Turtle's Back: A Native American Year of Moons.* New York: Scholastic, Inc.
- Dixon, Ann. (2002). *Winter Is.* Portland, OR: Alaska Northwest Books.
- Keller, Laurie. (1998). *The Scrambled States of America.* New York: Scholastic, Inc.
- Lyon, George Ella. (2000). *One Lucky Girl.* New York: Dorling Kindersley Publishing, Inc.
- Seuling, Barbara. (1998). *Winter Lullaby.* San Diego: Browndeer Press.
- Seuling, Barbara. (2001). *Spring Song.* San Diego: Gulliver Books.
- Wallner, Alexandra. (2000). *Sergio and the Hurricane.* New York: Henry Holt and Company.
- Wright, Betty Ren. (2003). *The Blizzard.* New York: Holiday House.

## Ecosystems

The second text set, Ecosystems, is a large set with subsets identified within it. They are a mixture of fiction and nonfiction books. Some focus on humans in the environment, others focus on the flora and fauna. The smaller subsets are just a beginning place for an in-depth unit of study focused on a single ecosystem. The value of this full text set grouping is the ability to help students compare and contrast several ecosystems. Many students have not lived in other places nor traveled beyond their own communities. Nonfiction books provide visual and verbal information through photos, illustrations, diagrams, and text. Well-written and researched fictional books provide an opportunity for students to experience life in a different environment. Use these books to motivate student interest in the unit by starting with an interactive read-aloud followed by a discussion that generates a list of what students would like to know about the setting (environment) of the story.

### Ecosystems

#### *Arctic*

- Blake, Robert. (2002). *Togo.* New York: Philomel Books.
- Fowler, Susi Gregg. (1998). *Circle of Thanks.* New York: Scholastic, Inc.
- George, Jean Craighead. (1999). *Snow Bear.* New York: Hyperion Books for Children.

#### *Desert*

- Arnosky, Jim. (1998). *Watching Desert Wildlife.* Washington, D.C.: National Geographic Society.

- Asch, Frank. (1998). *Cactus Poems.* New York: Harcourt Brace & Co.
- Guiberson, Brenda Z. (1998). *Cactus Hotel.* New York: Scholastic, Inc.
- Johnston, Tony. (2000). *Desert Song.* San Francisco: Sierra Club Books for Children.
- Wright-Frierson, Virginia. (1996). *A Desert Scrapbook: Dawn to Dusk in the Sonoran Desert.* New York: Simon & Schuster Books for Young Readers.
- Yolen, Jane. (1996). *Welcome to the Sea of Sand.* New York: G. P. Putnam's Sons.

### Mountains

- Fourment, Tiffany. (2004). *My Water Comes from the Mountains.* Lanham, MD: Roberts Rinehart Publishers.
- Morris, Neil. (2005). *Living in the Mountains.* North Mankato, MN: Smart Apple Media.
- Nadeau, Isaac. (2006). *Mountains.* New York: The Rosen Publishing Group, Inc.

### Prairie

- Guiberson, Brenda Z. (1995). *Winter Wheat.* New York: Henry Holt and Company.
- Reynolds, Marilynn. (1999). *The Prairie Fire.* Victoria, B.C., Canada: Orca Book Publishers.
- Van Leeuwen, Jean. (1997). *A Fourth of July on the Plains.* New York: Dial Books for Young Readers.

### Rain Forest

- Cherry, Lynne. (2000). *The Great Kapok Tree: A Tale of the Amazon Rain Forest.* San Diego: Voyager Books Harcourt, Inc.
- Cherry, Lynne, and Plotkin, Mark J. (1998). *The Shaman's Apprentice: A Tale of the Amazon Rain Forest.* San Diego: A Gulliver Green Book.
- Kratter, Paul. (2004). *The Living Rain Forest: An Animal Alphabet.* Watertown, MA: Charlesbridge.
- Pirotta, Saviour. (1999). *Rivers in the Rain Forest.* Austin, TX: Raintree Steck-Vaugh Publishers.

### Rivers

- Cherry, Lynne. (1992). *A River Ran Wild.* San Diego: A Gulliver Green Book.
- Hiscock, Bruce. (1997). *The Big Rivers: The Missouri, the Mississippi, and the Ohio.* New York: Antheneum Books for Young Readers.
- Lourie, Peter. (2000). *Mississippi River: A Journey Down the Father of Waters.* Honesdale, PA: Boyds Mills Press.

### Swamp

- Arnosky, Jim. (2000). *Wild and Swampy.* New York: HarperCollins Publishers.
- Guiberson, Brenda Z. (1992). *Spoonbill Swamp.* New York: Henry Holt and Company.

*Other*

- George, Lindsay Barrett. (2006). *In the Garden: Who's Been Here?* New York: Greenwillow Books.
- Hubbell, Patricia. (2001). *Sea, Sand, Me!* New York: HarperCollins Publishers.
- Morpurgo, Michael. (2000). *Wombat Goes Walkabout.* Cambridge, MA: Candlewick Press.
- Root, Phyllis. (2004). *If You Want to See a Caribou.* Boston: Houghton Mifflin Co.
- Saul, Carol P. (1995). *Someplace Else.* New York: Simon & Schuster Books for Young Readers.
- Siebert, Diane. (2000). *Cave.* New York: HarperCollins Publishers.
- Van Leeuwen, Jean. (1998). *Nothing Here but Trees:* New York: Dial Books for Young Readers.

## Teaching Ideas—Lesson Plans and Extension/Application Activities

*Planet Earth/Inside Out* by Gail Gibbons was used as the beginning point in a third-grade study of Earth's systems and cycles. This lesson, with discussion prompted by the text and teacher-prepared questions, was a way to learn what the students already knew. These students were not familiar with the use of an Anticipation/Reaction guide, so it was necessary to thoroughly explain the instructions.

## Lesson Plan 3.1—Planet Earth/Inside Out

### LEVEL: GRADE 2 (INTRODUCTORY), GRADES 3 AND 4 (REVIEW)

### Learning Goals

- Students will assess their knowledge of Earth facts before and after reading a book.
- Students will define and locate equator, North and South Poles, continents, and oceans on a map or globe.

### Assessment

- Informal assessment: Observation of discussion during interactive read aloud, particularly students' vocabulary choices.
- Formal assessment: Anticipation/Reaction Guide for *Planet Earth/Inside Out*. (Anecdotal notes about number correct in the After Reading column and analysis of which questions were answered incorrectly.)

### Materials

- *Planet Earth/Inside Out* by Gail Gibbons
- Anticipation/Reaction guide
- Overhead transparency of the Anticipation/Reaction guide

### Key Questions and/or Vocabulary

- sphere: a ball
- atmosphere: the gases and other materials that surround Earth and is held close by gravity
- equator: an imaginary line running east and west around the globe that is equidistant from the north and south poles
- continent: large land mass surrounded by oceans
- oceans: large body of salt water that separates continents
- rotate/rotation: the spinning of Earth on its axis
- revolve/revolution: the movement of Earth as it orbits the sun
- fossils: remains or impression of plant or animal hardened in rock

### Procedure

#### Motivation and Explanation

- State, "Today we are going to share one of my favorite books about Earth. It contains lots of interesting information. Before we read the book, think about what you already know about Earth."
- Pass out the Anticipation/Reaction guide.
- Help students fold the guide on the two vertical dotted lines. Move around the room to assist anyone who has problems with the folding.

#### Demonstration and Modeling

- Show the students your guide. Demonstrate how the questions remain visible but the lines before and after the statements can be hidden by folding back that part of the guide.

- Have the students fold back the right side (After Reading side) so that just the Before Reading and the statements show.
- Read the first statement aloud from the overhead projector. Think aloud as you consider whether you agree or disagree with the statement. Tell the students that this process is like predicting; they should use what they know to answer the question but not worry about right or wrong answers.

### Guided Practice

- Have students mark "agree or disagree" next to the first statement on their guides.
- Read each of the statements as students agree or disagree under the Before Reading column.
- Have students gather together on the floor after they finish, and read the book. Remind them to listen for information in the book that will tell them if the statements on the guide are right or wrong.
- Encourage students to interact with the information in the text. Allow them to make references to content related to the statements on the guide.

### Independent Practice

- Have students return to their desks when reading and discussion have finished.
- Tell them to fold the Before Reading column behind the statements so that just the statements and After Reading column shows. Now they are going to reread the seven statements and agree or disagree based on what they learned from the book.
- Read the statements to students if they have difficulty reading independently, but do not engage in any conversation.

### Closure/Reflection

- Place the transparency on the overhead projector. Have students show all parts of the guide. Read the statements again and tell them to decide what answers should be.
- Do not allow the students to change their original responses on the guide as you read the statements and they provide the answers. After reading each statement again, find the place in the text that confirms or denies the statement. If the text disagrees, ask students how to change the statement so that it agrees with the text.
- Model on the overhead projector. For example: "1. Earth is the fifth planet from the sun." Cross out *fifth* and write *third* above it. Now the statement reads: "Earth is the third planet from the sun." This is a true statement.
- Continue until all seven statements have been read and corrected, as needed.

Day and night and the seasons are part of Earth's systems and cycles. Despite learning in first grade about Earth spinning on its axis to produce day and night, some students need to review the concept again in third grade. Remember that they may not be able to think abstractly about everything, so concrete models and a periodic review of the concepts are helpful.

Clarify that although the earth is tilted toward the sun during summer, it is not closer to the sun. The warmer temperatures are due to the angle at which the rays of sunshine strike Earth. The portion of the earth (either Northern or Southern Hemisphere) tilted toward the sun is warmer because the angle of the rays is more direct. In the winter the angles are not as direct.

## *Lesson Plan 3.2—Reasons for Seasons*

### LEVEL: KINDERGARTEN AND GRADE 1 (WHOLE GROUP TREE IN SEASONS ACTIVITY) GRADES 2 AND 3

### Learning Goals

- Students will explain the cause of day and night.
- Students will explain the cause of seasons.
- Students will describe the characteristics of the seasons.

### Assessment

- Informal assessment: Observation of discussion during read-aloud.
- Formal assessment: Tree in Seasons handout
- Predetermined assessment:

  - +5—several details added to the tree in each season; accurate facts about the season
  - +3—some details added to the tree in each season; most facts about season included and accurate
  - +1—parts of tree drawings are missing; few or incorrect facts

### Materials

- *On Earth* by Brian G. Karas
- Tree in Seasons overhead transparency
- Tree in Seasons worksheet
- crayons—pink, green, red, brown, orange
- Reason for Seasons informational handout
- globe

### Key Questions and/or Vocabulary

- rotate/rotation: the spinning of Earth on its axis
- revolve/revolution: the movement of Earth as it orbits the sun
- orbit: the path of Earth's revolution around the sun
- tilt: the angle of Earth on its axis
- hemisphere: Northern and Southern

### Procedure

#### *Motivation and Explanation*

- Provide each student with a copy of the Tree in Seasons worksheet as you put the overhead transparency on the overhead projector. Students need to pull out their crayons.
- Have students note that there are four sections and four illustrations of the same tree. Tell students that you are going to tell about the life of a tree on this paper.
- Using a brown overhead marker, color the trunk and branches of each tree. Have the students do the same.

- Begin with the tree in the top left quadrant. Tell the children that you are going to put pink dots on the branches of this tree. Ask what they think these dots are (blossoms). Ask students to look at the arrows on the page, and tell you where to go next.
- Move to the top right quadrant. Draw many green leaves on the branches of this tree.
- Move to the bottom right quadrant. Draw red dots, some green leaves, and some orange leaves on the tree, and draw some green leaves and some orange leaves on the ground. Ask: "What are the red dots? Why are the leaves green and orange? Why are some leaves on the ground?"
- Leave the tree in the bottom left quadrant just as it is.
- Ask students to look at the life of the tree they have created. What can they tell about it? If they do not comment about the seasons, guide students to match seasons to the various parts of the tree's life. Ask students what are some characteristics of the four seasons.
- Remind students that people are in many different locations on Earth. What do they think the seasons are like in the Arctic? What about Florida? What about at the equator?
- Record the season names and characteristics on the overhead. Read a book about the seasons to see if anything was left out of the students' discussion.

### Demonstration and Modeling

- Gather students on the floor to read the book.
- Refer to the overhead drawing of the tree and your class notes while reading.
- Use the globe to reinforce the image when the book discusses the tilt of the earth. Also, include the spin (rotation) of the earth creating day and night as well as the revolution around the sun to mark a year.
- Examine Earth's orbit and the tilt and be sure students locate the United States on the globe—in the Northern Hemisphere—and Australia in the Southern Hemisphere. Mention that when one country is experiencing a season, the other country is experiencing the opposite season. Note that the opposite seasons are diagonally across from each other on the Tree in Seasons handout.

### Guided Practice

- Have students return to their desks and examine the Tree in Seasons worksheet. Discuss what should be added to the previous notes, and what should be changed or removed.
- Distribute the Reasons for Seasons handout. Have students put an X on the Northern Hemisphere on each Earth symbol. Together, determine in which position the United States (in the Northern Hemisphere) is experiencing winter.

### Independent Practice

- Have students identify the positions for summer, fall, and spring.

### Closure/Reflection

- Have students define and demonstrate rotate and revolve and how each affects people on Earth.

- Ask students to share why they looked at the life of a tree when they were learning about the seasons.
- Ask questions such as, "What effect does the change in season have on you? What season are we currently in? How will life change for us as we move to the next season? Do all people on Earth have the same experiences with seasons?"

## *Extension/Application Activity 3.1—Water Cycle*

### LEVEL: GRADE 2 (INTRODUCTORY), GRADE 3 (REVIEW)

- Review or teach the water cycle. Use *My Water Comes from the Mountains* by Tiffany Fourment.
- Share Neil Waldman's *Snowflake* during a read-aloud. Discuss how his story and illustrations look at precipitation in multiple forms over a year, and state that they are the result of differences in temperature. List the forms of precipitation in the book.
- Have students create a chart that considers forms of precipitation in each of the seasons and what conditions are needed to create that form.

First-grade students must be able to gather and classify information on climate, location, and physical surroundings, and tell how they affect the way people meet their basic needs. The unit begins with *The Scrambled States of America,* a delightful tale of a party orchestrated by the states of Kansas and Nebraska, who are bored. The celebration is so successful that the newly acquainted states decide to do some relocation. They discover, much to their dismay, that they are not prepared to live in a new location. The book is a perfect way to introduce the impact of location, climate, and physical surroundings on meeting basic needs.

## *Lesson Plan 3.3—Scrambled States of America*

### LEVEL: GRADES 1 AND 2

### Learning Goals

- Students will examine state locations on a map.
- Students will identify state locations in relationship to the North Pole and equator.
- Students will compare and contrast climatic characteristics of states in terms of their relationship to the North Pole and equator.

### Assessment

- Informal assessment: Observation of discussion, particularly noticing connections between climate/temperatures to location related to North Pole and equator.

### Materials

- *The Scrambled States of America* by Laurie Keller
- *America the Beautiful* illustrated by Neil Waldman
- United States map
- world map

### Key Questions and/or Vocabulary

- location: the position of a place on Earth
- weather: day-to-day temperature and precipitation conditions
- climate: long-term trends in weather

### Procedure

#### *Motivation and Explanation*

- Ask students if they have lived or traveled in a place that was different from where they now live. Discuss the various places they name.
- Use the United States map to locate where the school is located. Name the state and city/town. As students share the names/places they visit, locate them on the map.
- Briefly share *America the Beautiful*. Note the various locations identified—desert, waterfalls, plains, mountains. Consider weather/climate in these locations.
- Ask, "What do you think would happen if the states changed their locations?" Accept predictions and then read the book. As you read, indicate the various states on the map. Make certain that students understand that this is a fictional story.

#### *Demonstration and Modeling*

- Finish reading and say, "I noticed the states were not ready to move to another location. Look at page (show the page). Florida was freezing and Minnesota got sunburned. Do you think it has something to do with where the states are located?" Look at the United States map and note that Florida is in the south and Minnesota is in the north.

### *Guided Practice*

- Ask students why being north or south matters. Encourage students to think about the location of the United States in the world. Display the world map.
- Lead students in a discussion about temperatures at the equator and how they change as we move to one pole or the other, particularly if students do not use the North Pole and the equator as markers.
- Return to the United States map and discuss temperature differences based on location.
- Ask students whether there are other problems related to the relocation. Accept answers/examples.

### *Closure/Reflection*

- Tell students they are going to learn about other places in the country, and ask whether they think that will include discussing locations.
- Ask the following questions: "If we decided to take a trip to Alaska, what might we want to pack for our trip? Why? Do you think we might eat different food or see different plants and animals in Alaska? Why?"
- Read a book about a child who lives in the Arctic.

    NOTE: *The Scrambled States of America* is also available on video streaming.

The lesson following *The Scrambled States of America* is based on a read-aloud experience with *Snow Bear* by Jean Craighead George. One of this story's unique features is the parallel text. George describes Vincent's protection of Bessie, as well as the mother polar bear's protection of Snow Bear, their parallel actions, and the actions of Bessie and Snow Bear. This is similar to the parallel text in Robert McCloskey's classic *Blueberries for Sal. Snow Bear* is a simple story, but with the addition of illustrations, first graders can discern characteristics unique to the Arctic. Fowler's *Circle of Thanks* might be substituted because it follows a full year and introduces more information about indigenous animals. Select a book that provides the level of information your students need.

## *Extension/Application Activity 3.2—Compare/Contrast Environments Chart*

### LEVEL: KINDERGARTEN (WHOLE GROUP CHART ONLY) GRADES 1 AND 2

- Engage the students in an interactive read-aloud; then have them return to their seats and introduce the chart (See Figure 3.1). Prepare the chart on white butcher paper, creating large boxes to record data. Provide each student with a copy of the chart for personal recording. Note that the teacher's model chart and the student's charts should not include the information in the parentheses on the following chart. These are the teacher's talking points for the discussions with the students as the chart is completed together.
- Begin by discussing where the Arctic is located. Guide students to think about the North Pole. In the location box draw a diagram of Earth on its axis. You might add a squiggly line to create land around the pole area and an arrow that labels the pole. Draw and label the equator. Include a compass rose in the box with only N indicated.

- Use words like snowy and cold in the Climate box. Encourage the students to remember the clothing Bessie and Vincent wore. Include drawings of long-sleeved, hooded parkas, snow pants, and boots.
- Define the word *surroundings* as you begin to complete this box. Draw ice mountains and a snowflake to represent snow. Since the book was limited to polar bears and does not include plants, draw only a polar bear unless the students have more information.
- Consider how Vincent would obtain food; for example, he carries a gun in the story. Discuss the proximity to water, leading students to consider that Bessie and Vincent ate fish. The food box in the chart may be somewhat limited because the text is limited.
- Revisit the chart as you read about the desert using *A Desert Scrapbook: Dawn to Dusk in the Sonoran Desert* by Virginia Wright Frierson, and show photos from *Cactus Poems* by Frank Asch and Ted Levin. Another interesting book to use in this lesson is *Someplace Else* by Carol Saul.
- Make adaptations based on your curriculum, such as what books to use to represent the ecosystem, the content of the chart for comparisons, and how teacher-directed the lesson will be. This sample lesson was used with first graders who were experiencing these concepts for the first time and who required more direction. With an older or experienced group of students, model and guide and then allow them time for independent practice.

Compare and Contrast Environment Chart

|  | Arctic | Desert | Mountains | Home State |
|---|---|---|---|---|
| **Location** (region, place on the earth, etc.) |  |  |  |  |
| **Climate** (temperature, clothing demands) |  |  |  |  |
| **Surroundings** (landforms, plants, and animals) |  |  |  |  |
| **Food** (crops harvested, source of meat, etc.) |  |  |  |  |

**Figure 3.1** Compare/Contrast Environments Chart.

## *Extension/Application Activity 3.3—Compare/Contrast Environments Book*
### LEVEL: GRADES 1, 2, AND 3

- Prepare a Dos-a-Dos for those students who are independent workers and want a research challenge.

- Allow students to select two environments to be compared. Data about one environment will be collected in one side of the book and data about the other environment will be collected in the other side of the book.
- Title each page within the books with the categories of information to be collected. For example: Location, Climate, Surroundings, and Foods used in the chart in Activity 3.1., or generate another category list.
- Provide students with a variety of resource books and access to the school library to conduct research.
- Provide art materials for students to decorate the covers after all the data has been collected.
- Share the completed books.

## Review Activity—Cootie Catcher

### LEVEL: GRADES 2, 3, AND 4

Create academic "cootie catchers" to make homework more interesting

### *Preparing the Cootie Catcher*

1. Enlarge the reproducible so that the Cootie Catcher square measures 8" x 8".
2. Cut on the solid lines producing a square cootie catcher and a rectangular "cheat sheet."
3. Crease all dotted lines.
4. Fold the "cootie catcher" according to the following steps:

   - With written-side up, fold under the four corners.
   - With picture-side down and word-side up, fold the four corners forward; you should see pictures only.
   - Fold in half, once each direction to make it more flexible; the pictures should be hidden.

5. Insert index finger and thumb in each pocket. The words should show.

### *Rules for Playing Cootie Catcher Review Activity*

1. Pair students.
2. One student manipulates the cootie catcher while the other takes a turn (the player).
3. The player selects one of the words and spells it while the manipulator opens and closes the cootie catcher, alternating directions.
4. The player now selects one of the pictures and spells the vocabulary word it represents (can use the cheat sheet) while the manipulator again opens and closes the cootie catcher.
5. The player selects one of the pictures, then the manipulator lifts the picture and asks the question under the picture.
6. The player receives one point for each correct answer.
7. The winner is the one with the most points.
8. Students switch roles and play again.

# Planet Earth/Inside Out
by Gail Gibbons
1995 – Morrow Junior Books/New York

## An Anticipation/Reaction Guide

<u>BEFORE READING</u>
Agree  Disagree

<u>AFTER READING</u>
Agree  Disagree

_____ _____   1. Earth is the fifth planet from the sun.   _____ _____

_____ _____   2. Sunlight shining on the water covering much of the planet gives Earth its blue color.   _____ _____

_____ _____   3. The bulge at the middle of Earth is called the equator.   _____ _____

_____ _____   4. The four oceans on Earth's surface are the Arctic, Indian, Atlantic, and Pacific.   _____ _____

_____ _____   5. The sun warms the Earth more strongly at the North and South Poles.   _____ _____

_____ _____   6. Fossils are studied to help us understand how life on Earth has changed.   _____ _____

_____ _____   7. People have abused Earth's natural resources, and some of Earth's environment has been damaged.   _____ _____

Take care of the Earth every day.

From *Shaped by the Standards: Geographic Literacy Through Children's Literature* by Linda K. Rogers. Westport, CT: Teacher Ideas Press/Libraries Unlimited. Copyright © 2008.

Sabbatical 2007 – L.K. Rogers

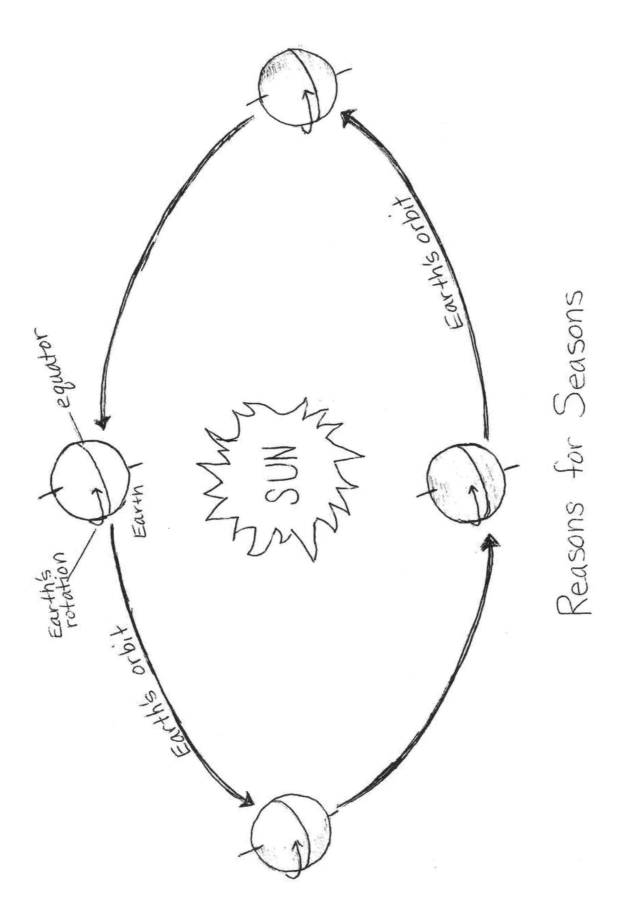

Reasons for Seasons

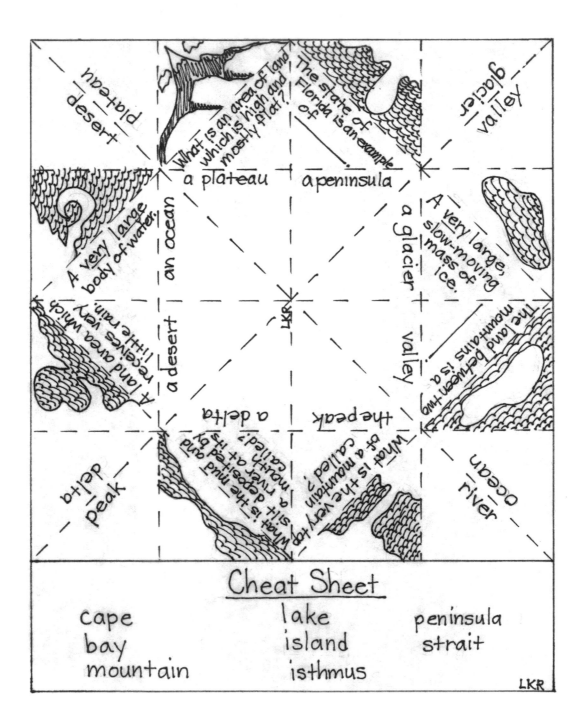

desert plateau

What is an area of land which is high and mostly flat?

The state of Florida is an example of

glacier valley

a plateau     a peninsula

A very large body of water.

an ocean

a glacier

A very large, slow-moving mass of ice.

A land area which receives very little rain.

a desert

The land between two mountains is a

valley

a delta     the peak

delta peak

What is the mud and silt deposited by a river at its mouth called?

What is the very top of a mountain called?

river ocean

## Cheat Sheet

| cape | lake | peninsula |
| bay | island | strait |
| mountain | isthmus | |

LKR

From *Shaped by the Standards: Geographic Literacy Through Children's Literature* by Linda K. Rogers. Westport, CT: Teacher Ideas Press/Libraries Unlimited. Copyright © 2008.

## Dos a Dos: Dialog Journal

(Based on *BookArts* handout, Dr. Patricia Pinciotti, East Stroudsburg University of Pennsylvania)

Dos a Dos is a French expression meaning a couch or a carriage that holds two people sitting back to back. When two people sit back to back they see different things or they see the same thing from different points of view. This book is really two books in one. There is room for each person's point of view or story.

Dos a dos can be a wonderful way to structure a dialog journal where you and another person write back and forth to each other. Each person has his/her own book and in turn responds to the other's ideas, questions, and feelings. Turn them around and read each other's response. Or, use the dos a dos to create a journal in two voices. Write as one person or character in one book and another person or character in the other book.

### Directions

**Step 1:**
Use a piece of 12" × 18" construction paper. Cut it lengthwise in half (making two 6" × 18" pieces). Fold one strip into three equal pieces. It should look like a Z. This becomes the cover for both books—they share a common "back."

**Step 2:**
Use 8 ½" × 11" paper to create the booklet or signature to insert within the covers. Cut the paper so that it is 5 ½" × 8 ½". Fold them in half. Divide them in half so that you have a booklet or signature for each book.

**Step 3:**
Insert a signature into one fold of the cover. It should be nested inside the crease. You can either staple the signature into the cover or sew it to the cover. The simplest way is to staple the booklet in by using a book arm stapler that lets you staple deep into the center of the signature. Or, you can use a hole punch to put a hole through the cover and signature pages at the top and bottom of the crease. Then tie the pages together using yarn or embroidery floss.

**Step 4:**
Repeat Step 3 for the other signature, nesting it in the other crease.

**Step 5:**
Fold the book back and fourth so you can open one signature from the front and one from the back.

**Step 6:**
Decorate the covers.

**Variations:**
- Put lined paper in one book and unlined paper in the other so that the responses can be verbal and visual.
- Change the size, shape, and materials to suit your need.

## CHAPTER 4

# Human Systems

Physical and human phenomena are spatially distributed over Earth's surface. The outcome of *Geography for Life* is a geographically informed person (1) who sees meaning in the arrangement of things in space; (2) who sees relations between people, places, and environments; (3) who uses geographic skills; and (4) who applies spatial and ecological perspectives to life situations.

**HUMAN SYSTEMS**

People are central to geography in that human activities help shape Earth's surface, human settlements and structures are part of Earth's surface, and humans compete for control of Earth's surface.

The geographically informed person knows and understands:

9. The characteristics, distribution, and migration of human populations on Earth's surface.
   a. The spatial distribution of population.
   b. The characteristics of populations at different scales (local to global).
   c. The causes and effects of human migration.

10. The characteristics, distribution, and complexity of Earth's cultural mosaics.
    a. How the characteristics of culture affect the way in which people live.
    b. How patterns of culture vary across Earth's surface.
    c. How cultures change.

11. The patterns and networks of economic interdependence on Earth's surface.
    a. The location and spatial distribution of economic activities.
    b. The factors that influence the location and spatial distribution of economic activities.
    c. The transportation and communication networks used in daily life.

12. The processes, patterns, and functions of human settlement.
    a. The types and spatial patterns of settlement.
    b. The factors that affect where people settle.
    c. How spatial patterns of human settlement change.
    d. The spatial characteristics of cities.

13. How the forces of cooperation and conflict among people influence the division and control of Earth's surface.
    a. The types of territorial units.
    b. The extent and characteristics of political, social, and economic units at different scales (local and global).

c. How people divide Earth's surface.

d. How cooperation and conflict affect places in the local community.

*Geography for Life: National Geography Standards* (National Council for the Social Studies, 1994, pp. 35, 122–131).

This essential element, *Human Systems,* includes five standards—the most, by far, in any essential element. The statement under this element recognizes the centrality of humans to geography as students consider how human activities help shape Earth's surface, that human settlements and structures are part of Earth's surface, and that humans compete for control of Earth's surface.

The number of books identified with this essential element for text sets is also larger than any other. Perhaps this is because children's literature is often concerned with people and their stories, and this group of standards examines the characteristics of humans. These standards clearly represent the Theme of Movement.

## Text Sets—Exploration, Immigration, Westward Expansion, Underground Railroad, Cultural Mosaics, Transportation, Civil War, Revolutionary War, World War II

Standard 9 considers the migration of humans on Earth's surface. Several of the text sets in this chapter deal with this issue: Exploration, Immigration, Underground Railroad, and Westward Expansion. Books in the Exploration text set examine more global events, and Immigration, Underground Railroad, and Westward Expansion focus on migration affecting the United States.

### *Exploration*

The Exploration text set contains the accounts of two explorers who predate Marco Polo. These two books, *Traveling Man: The Journey of Ibn Battuta, 1325–1354* and *The Travels of Benjamin of Tudela: Through Three Continents in the Twelfth Century* are not particularly student-friendly for primary students, but they can broaden the teacher's background and be intriguing to mature fourth graders. The most modern of explorers is Neil Armstrong—although his exploration as the first human on the moon did not take place on Earth's surface. He is also included in the Transportation text set.

The three books about the Lewis and Clark Expedition document the extraordinary early nineteenth-century journey that opened up the North American continent. Two of the books are relatively new, obviously published to coincide with the 200th anniversary of the expedition. Set in the late nineteenth century, Don Brown celebrates Mary Kingsley's adventures in Africa, and Alice Provensen looks at the story of one explorer, an adventurer/prospector, who took on the wilds of Alaska to discover gold.

Readers will find *The Explorer's Gazette* charming. This clever presentation of explorers across time reveals some little-known explorers. Also, why not use the newspaper format for students' explorer report? The whimsy of *So You Want to Be an Explorer?* is sure to catch the attention of students. St. George cleverly arranges the explorers in thought-provoking groups as she romps through history. Lewin offers a beautifully illustrated retelling of the discovery of Machu Picchu in 1911 by explorer Hiram Bingham.

## Exploration

- Adler, David A. (2003). *A Picture Book of Lewis and Clark.* New York: Holiday House.
- Blumberg, Rhoda (2004). *York's Adventures with Lewis and Clark: An African-American's Part in the Great Expedition.* New York: HarperCollins Publishers.
- Brown, Don. (1998). *One Giant Leap: The Story of Neil Armstrong.* Boston: Houghton Mifflin Company.
- Brown, Don. (2000). *Uncommon Traveler: Mary Kingsley in Africa.* New York: Houghton Mifflin Company.
- Heckscher, Melissa, Shulman, Mark, and the Staff of the Explorer's Gazette. (2004). *The Explorer's Gazette.* New York: Tangerine Press.
- Lewin, Ted. (2003). *Lost City: The Discovery of Machu Picchu.* New York: Philomel Books.
- Provensen, Alice. (2005). *Klondike Gold.* New York: Simon & Schuster Books for Young Readers.
- Rumford, James. (2001). *Traveling Man: The Journey of Ibn Battuta, 1325–1354.* Boston: Houghton Mifflin Company.
- St. George, Judith. (2005). *So You Want to Be an Explorer?* New York: Philomel Books.
- Schanzer, Rosalyn. (1997). *How We Crossed the West: The Adventures of Lewis and Clark.* New York: Scholastic, Inc.
- Shulevitz, Uri. (2005). *The Travels of Benjamin of Tudela: Through Three Continents in the Twelfth Century.* New York: Farrar Straus Giroux.
- Yolen, Jane. (1996). *Encounter.* San Diego: Harcourt Brace & Company.

## *Immigration*

The collection of books in the Immigration text set looks at past immigration stories related to the Pilgrim's experience and Ellis Island, as well as a modern look at immigration.

As a child, I was always disappointed that I could not claim a unique nationality. My father always told us we were Americans. No one in our family had immigrated to the United States for generations. But when my children were small, I discovered that my family members are descendents of the Mayflower through my paternal grandfather. Indeed, my father was right. I am a fourteenth-generation descendent of Isaac Allerton, one of the original Pilgrims. My children and I did a little research about Isaac Allerton, and I was delighted and amazed to realize that I had taught about this ancestor when I began teaching third grade! The story of the Allertons is also recounted in *Three Young Pilgrims* by Cheryl Harness. Other Pilgrim-related books in this text set are Bruchac's story of Squanto, Carol Crane's alphabet book about Thanksgiving, and Melmed's Thanksgiving counting book.

Maestro shares the history of immigration in this country. *The Memory Coat, Journey to Ellis Island, Landed,* and *Coming to America* are the more typical look back at past immigration stories. *Together in Pinecone Patch* is set in the past; however, the story's focus is the conflict between two immigrant groups in the new country who have more in common than they realize. Two Chinese brothers tell their story in the context of the building of the transcontinental railroad in *Coolies.* Younger brother, Ming, arrives in San Francisco after his older brothers have established a family store in *Brothers,* a sequel to *Coolies.*

Immigration is a dynamic that is not just about the past, as is sometimes implied by the content taught. As schools reflect a more diverse student body, the more that modern immigration stories can help educate students and possibly ease some of the adjustments.

Aliki, Bunting, Kurtz, Park, Perez, and Say tell modern-day immigration stories. Marianthe, in Aliki's story, struggles with communication as does Farah in *One Green Apple.* Both girls begin to feel a connection to their new school setting. Desta, in *Faraway Home,* is concerned that her father might not want to return to the United States when he goes to Ethiopia to visit his family and former homeland. May, in Say's *Tea with Milk,* is caught between two cultures. Bunting tells the touching story of David who is afraid of changes to his American family as he and his parents await the arrival of an adopted baby, Jin Woo, from Korea. Through a fictionalized diary account, Perez shares her personal experience of leaving her extended family and the culture she knew in Mexico for a new life with her parents and siblings in the United States. The Parks tell the story of Jangmi who prepares to move from Korea to Massachusetts. Despite some of the fears and sorrow for what she is leaving, her parents' enthusiasm helps her look forward to the move.

## Immigration

- Aliki. (1998). *Marianthe's Story: Painted Words; Marianthe's Story: Spoken Memories.* New York: Greenwillow Books.
- Bierman, Carol. (1998). *Journey to Ellis Island: How My Father Came to America.* Toronto: Madison Press Books.
- Bruchac, Joseph. (2000). *Squanto's Journey: The Story of the First Thanksgiving.* San Diego: Silver Whistle–Harcourt, Inc.
- Bunting, Eve. (2001). *Jin Woo.* New York: Clarion Books.
- Bunting, Eve. (2006). *One Green Apple.* New York: Clarion Books.
- Crane, Carol. (2003). *P Is for Pilgrim: A Thanksgiving Alphabet.* Chelsea, MI: Sleeping Bear Press.
- Harness, Cheryl. (1995). *Three Young Pilgrims.* New York: Aladdin Paperbacks.
- Kurtz, Jane. (2000). *Faraway Home.* San Diego: Gulliver Books.
- Lee, Millie. (2006). *Landed.* New York: Frances Foster Books.
- Maestro, Betsy. (1996). *Coming to America: The Story of Immigration.* New York: Scholastic, Inc.

- Melmed, Laura Krauss. (2001). *This First Thanksgiving Day: A Counting Story.* New York: HaperCollins Publishers.
- Park, Frances, and Park, Ginger. (2002). *Good-bye, 382 Shin Dang Dong.* Washington, D.C.: National Geographic Society.
- Perez, Amada Irma. (2002). *My Diary from Here to There.* San Francisco: Children's Book Press.
- Say, Allen. (1999). *Tea with Milk.* Boston: Houghton Mifflin Company.
- Schanzer, Rosalyn. (2000). *Escaping to America: A True Story.* New York: Harper-Collins Publishers.
- Thompson, Gare. (1997). *Immigrants: Coming to America.* New York: Children's Press.
- Woodruff, Elvira. (1999). *The Memory Coat.* New York: Scholastic Press.
- Yezerski, Thomas. (1998). *Together in Pinecone Patch.* New York: Farrar, Straus and Giroux.
- Yin. (2000). *Coolies.* New York: Philomel Books.
- Yin. (2006). *Brothers.* New York: Philomel Books.

## Westward Expansion

The migration across the country during the 1800s after the Lewis and Clark Expedition is commonly taught as the westward expansion to settle new lands. Five of the books are the more traditional story: *When Pioneer Wagons Rumbled West, You Wouldn't Want to Be an American Pioneer!: A Wilderness You'd Rather Not Tame, Yippee-Yah!: A Book about Cowboys and Cowgirls, A Fourth of July on the Plains,* and *Nothing Here but Trees.*

Others books take a more unique approach. Hopkinson uses a tall-tale format to tell how the first apples arrived in Oregon. Provensen's Alaskan gold-rush story reminds us of how many people became residents of our most northern state. *I Have Heard of a Land* recognizes that the land rush was for all people including women and blacks. Bunting's *Train to Somewhere* is a poignant story about the orphan trains that functioned in the late 1800s into the twentieth century. Devised as a way to move orphans out of New York City orphanages, these trains made trips across the country into the Midwest, stopping along the way for children to be adopted.

### Westward Expansion

- Bunting, Eve. (1996). *Train to Somewhere.* New York: Scholastic, Inc.
- Gibbons, Gail. (1999). *Yippee-Yah!: A Book about Cowboys and Cowgirls.* Boston: Little, Brown and Company.
- Graham, Christine. (1997). *When Pioneer Wagons Rumbled West.* Salt Lake City, Utah: Shadow Mountain.
- Hopkinson, Deborah. (2004). *Apples to Oregon.* New York: An Anne Schwartz Book.
- Morley, Jacqueline. (2002). *You Wouldn't Want to Be an American Pioneer!: A Wilderness You'd Rather Not Tame.* New York: Franklin Watts.

- Provensen, Alice. (2005). *Klondike Gold.* New York: Simon & Schuster Books for Young Readers.
- Thomas, Joyce Carol. (1998). *I Have Heard of a Land.* New York: Joanna Cotler Books.
- Van Leeuwen, Jean. (1997). *A Fourth of July on the Plains.* New York: Dial Books for Young Readers.
- Van Leeuwen, Jean. (1998). *Nothing Here but Trees.* New York: Dial Books for Young Readers.

## *Underground Railroad*

An amazing number of beautifully illustrated books tell the story of the Underground Railroad that supported the migration of thousands of American slaves from pre-Civil War southern states to northern states and Canada. Harriet Tubman, a freed slave, was an extraordinary woman. Called Moses for her role in leading an enslaved people, Tubman and her story are found in Ringgold's and Weatherford's unique books. Weatherford's story focuses on Tubman's strong faith and may not be appropriate for all settings, but it should be read by teachers. Hopkinson, Stroud, and Woodson involve the use of quilts as maps in their stories about this northern migration. Ransom sets her story in Fredericksburg, Virginia, to help the reader understand that slaves lived and served in places other than plantations.

### Underground Railroad

- Hopkinson, Deborah. (2002). *Under the Quilt of Night.* New York: Scholastic, Inc.
- Nelson, Vaunda Micheaux. (2003). *Almost to Freedom.* New York: Scholastic, Inc.
- Ransom, Candice. (2003). *Liberty Street.* New York: Walker & Company.
- Ringgold, Faith. (1995). *Aunt Harriet's Underground Railroad in the Sky.* New York: Crown.
- Stroud, Bettye. (2005). *The Patchwork Path: A Quilt Map to Freedom.* Cambridge, MA: Candlewick Press.
- Weatherford, Carole Boston. (2006). *Moses: When Harriet Tubman Led Her People to Freedom.* New York: Hyperion Books for Children.
- Woodson, Jacqueline. (2005). *Show Way.* New York: G. P. Putnam's Sons.

## *Cultural Mosaics*

The Cultural Mosaics text set has three subsets. Within the Distribution subset are two themes. One is the physical evidence of human distribution in the faces of humans. *I Saw Your Face* is a lyrical poem that accompanies exquisite drawings of children's faces taken from award-winning artist Tom Feeling's sketchbooks. The words and drawings document the African diaspora. It is joined with the other books celebrating the "colors of the earth" by Hamanaka, Katz, and Pinkney. *The Spice Alphabet Book* and *Circle Unbroken* look at cultural evidence carried from one place to another. Smith and Steele provide statistics to document our distribution on Earth's surface.

The Native American subset looks at ancient and modern Native Americans. Of particular note are Lorenz's and Littlechild's works. Lorenz uses anthropological findings to create an intriguing look at a rich Native American culture in thirteenth-century North America. Littlechild shares his challenges and celebrations as a modern day Native American artist. Most of his essays are not appropriate for K–4 students, but this book provides great insight for teachers.

The Other subset includes three great books. Ted Lewin's *Market!* shows the universal economic activity of marketing in multiple settings. *It's Disgusting* is a romp through the history of what humans have eaten and do eat; students will love it. Ammon's gentle tale of *An Amish Christmas* gives a glimpse into this unique rural culture.

## Cultural Mosaics

Refer to Chapter 2 Text Sets for Asia and Africa Distribution

- Dawes, Kwame. (2005). *I Saw Your Face.* New York: Dial Books.
- Hamanaka, Sheila. (1994). *All the Colors of the Earth.* New York: Scholastic, Inc.
- Katz, Karen. (1999). *The Colors of Us.* New York: Scholastic, Inc.
- Pallotta, Jerry. (1994). *The Spice Alphabet Book.* Watertown, MA: Charlesbridge.
- Pinkney, Sandra L. (2000). *Shades of Black: A Celebration of Our Children.* New York: Scholastic, Inc.
- Raven, Margot Theis. (2004). *Circle Unbroken: The Story of a Basket and Its People.* New York: Melanie Kroupa Books.
- Smith, David J. (2002). *If the World Were a Village: A Book about the World's People.* Toronto, ON: Kids Can Press.
- Steele, Philip. (2005). *Population Growth.* North Mankato, MN: Smart Apple Media.

## *Native American*

- Bruchac, Joseph. (2000). *Squanto's Journey: The Story of the First Thanksgiving.* San Diego: Silver Whistle–Harcourt, Inc.
- Bruchac, Joseph. (2004). *Many Nations: An Alphabet of Native America.* New York: Scholastic, Inc.
- Bruchac, Joseph and London, Jonathan. (1992). *Thirteen Moons on Turtle's Back: A Native American Year of Moons.* New York: Scholastic, Inc.
- Hoyt-Goldsmith, Diane. (1997). *Buffalo Days.* New York: Holiday House.
- Littlechild, George. (1993). *This Land Is My Land.* San Francisco: Children's Book Press.
- Lorenz, Albert with Schleh, Joy. (2003). *Journey to Cahokia: A Young Boy's Visit to the Great Mound City.* New York: Harry N. Abrams, Inc.
- Swamp, Chief Jake. (1997). *Giving Thanks: A Native American Good Morning Message.* New York: Scholastic, Inc.
- Wingate, Phillippa, and Struan Reid. (2003). *Who Were the First North Americans?* London: Usborne Publishing, Ltd.

## *Other*

- Ammon, Richard. (2000). *An Amish Christmas.* New York: Aladdin Paperbacks.
- Lewin, Ted. (1996). *Market!* New York: HarperCollins Publishers.
- Robson, Pam. (2005). *My Town.* Mankato, MN: Stargazer Books.
- Solheim, James. (1999). *It's Disgusting—And We Ate It!: True Food Facts from Around the World and Throughout History!* New York: Scholastic, Inc.


# *Transportation*

The study of transportation is common in the primary classroom. Geography Standard 11 connects this to economic interdependence. Transportation and its development are strongly related to exploration, immigration, and migration by humans across Earth's surface. As ability to transport has developed, humans are better able to reach remote places as they explore, immigrate, and migrate.

The books in this text set are subdivided by the areas that classroom teachers use: land, air, and water. Thompson's informational book is an overview of the development of transportation.

Man's great desire to fly is documented through Hansen's wonderful 190-page informational text—a great classroom resource. The other books in this category show the development of the hot air balloon, the Wright brother's contribution, and the contributions made by brave men like Lindbergh and Armstrong, and the fictional uncle in *wind flyers.* Pallotta and Stillwell's alphabet book offers the history of airplanes in a unique format.

Learners are certain to enjoy the books about *Alice Ramsey,* the first woman to drive across the United States in a car, and the Pony Express riders who delivered mail despite the dangers. The land subset also contains several books about trains and their impact on the nation and people. Two others, included because of their unique stories, are *Mailing May,* the imaginative yet true story of transporting a little girl to her grandmother's house in 1914; and *An Orange for Frankie* that demonstrates the difficulties our grandparents and great-grandparents had acquiring some of the food that we now take for granted. Simon's factual book about trucks and Weatherby's delightful fantasy about driving a big rig are perfect for primary students who love cars and trucks.


### Transportation

- Thompson, Gare. (1997). *Transportation: From Cars to Planes.* New York: Children's Press.

### *Air*

- Brown, Don. (1998). *One Giant Leap: The Story of Neil Armstrong.* Boston: Houghton Mifflin Company.
- Burleigh, Robert. (1991). *Flight: The Journey of Charles Lindbergh.* New York: Trumpet Club Special Edition.

- Busby, Peter. (2002). *First to Fly: How Wilber & Orville Wright Invented the Airplane.* Toronto: A Scholastic/Madison Press Book.
- Hansen, Ole Steen. (2003). *The Story of Flight.* New York: Crabtree Publishing Company.
- Johnson, Angela. (2007). *wind flyers.* New York: Simon & Schuster Books for Young Readers.
- Pallotta, Jerry, and Stillwell, Fred. (1997). *The Airplane Alphabet Book.* Watertown, MA: Charlesbridge.
- Priceman, Marjorie. (2005). *Hot Air: The (Mostly) True Story of the First Hot-Air Balloon Ride.* New York: Atheneum Books for Young Readers.
- Van Leeuwen, Jean. (2003). *The Amazing Air Balloon.* New York: Phyllis Fogelman Books.
- Yolen, Jane. (2003). *My Brothers' Flying Machine: Wilbur, Orville, and Me.* New York: Little, Brown and Company.

### *Land*

- Brown, Dan. (1997). *Alice Ramsey's Grand Adventure.* Boston: Houghton Mifflin, Co.
- Fuchs, Bernie. (2004). *Ride Like the Wind: A Tale of the Pony Express.* New York: The Blue Sky Press.
- Moss, Marissa. (1999). *True Heart.* San Diego: Silver Whistle.
- O'Brien, Patrick. (2000). *Steam, Smoke, and Steel: Back in Time with Trains.* New York: Charlesbridge Publishing.
- Polacco, Patricia. (2004). *An Orange for Frankie.* New York: Philomel Books.
- Simon, Seymour. (2000). *Seymour Simon's Book of Trucks.* New York: Simon & Schuster Books for Young Readers.
- Tunnell, Michael O. (1997). *Mailing May.* New York: Greenwillow Books.
- Weatherby, Brenda. (2004). *The Trucker.* New York: Scholastic Press.
- Yin. (2006). *Brothers.* New York: Philomel Books.

### *Water*

- Gilliland, Judith Heide. (2000). *Steamboat!: The Story of Captain Blanche Leathers.* New York: Dorling Kindersley Publishing, Inc.

Standard 13 reminds us that the division and control of Earth's surface involve both conflict and cooperation. Three text sets, each designated by a particular war, demonstrate the impact of conflict/war on children.

## *Civil War*

The Civil War text set offers three stories of drummer boys. Very young boys headed off to fight with no idea of what this act would mean. In *Pink and Say,* Polacco offers a touching story passed down through her family of two teenage Union soldiers whose lives intersect during the war.

### Civil War

- Bearden, Romare. (2003). *Li'l Dan the Drummer Boy: A Civil War Story.* New York: Simon & Schuster Books for Young Readers.
- Lewin, Ted. (2001). *Red Legs: A Drummer Boy of the Civil War.* New York: Harper-Collins Publisher.
- Noble, Trinka Hakes. (2006). *The Last Brother: A Civil War Tale.* Chelsea, MI: Sleeping Bear Press.
- Polacco, Patricia. (1995). *Pink and Say.* New York: Scholastic, Inc.
- Turner, Ann. (1998). *Drummer Boy.* New York: HarperCollins Publishers.

## Revolutionary War

The Revolutionary War text set includes three books that tell about particularly important events in the war: Lexington and Concord and crossing the Delaware River. Cheney and Peacock both emphasize the significance of Washington's action as he led his troops across the icy Delaware River. *The Scarlet Stocking* and *Sybil's Night Ride* showcase young heroines of the war while *Saving the Liberty Bell* is a lighthearted telling of a true event intended to fool the British.

### Revolutionary War

- Cheney, Lynne. (2004). *When Washington Crossed the Delaware: A Wintertime Story for Young Patriots.* New York: Simon & Schuster Books for Young Readers.
- Fradin, Dennis Brindell. (2005). *Let It Begin Here!: Lexington & Concord: First Battles of the American Revolution.* New York: Walker & Company.
- McDonald, Megan. (2005). *Saving the Liberty Bell.* New York: A Richard Jackson Book.
- Noble, Trinka Hakes. (2004). *The Scarlet Stocking Spy.* Chelsea, MI: Sleeping Bear Press.
- Peacock, Louise. (1998). *Crossing the Delaware: A History in Many Voices.* New York: Scholastic, Inc.
- Winnick, Karen B. (2000). *Sybil's Night Ride.* Honesdale, PA: Boyds Mills Press, Inc.

## World War II

The World War II text set includes two subsets, the European front and the Japanese-American Internment Camps. Borden's *Little Ships* is delightful and appropriate for all ages. *The Butterfly* and *Anne Frank* are beautiful picture books but have serious content that teachers need to address. Four other wonderful books whose appropriateness for students must also be carefully considered include *Luba: The Angel of Bergen-Belsen, Passage to Freedom: The Sugihara Story, Always Remember Me: How One Family Survived World War II,* and *The Orphans of Normandy: A True Story of World War II Told Through Drawings by Children.* Also highly recommended are *Fireflies in the Dark: The Story of Friedl Dicker-Brandeis and the Children of Terezin* for teachers only.

The Japanese-American internment camps are a sad part of American history. The books in this subset are beautiful and highly recommended for teachers. *So Far from the Sea* and *Flowers for Mariko* are perfect for third or fourth graders. Say's *Home of the Brave* is too abstract for K–4 students but certainly beautiful and haunting. Tunnell and Chilcoat's informational book about an internment camp in Utah is a mix of informational text and the voices of third-grade children.

## World War II

### *Europe*

- Amis, Nancy. (2003). *The Orphans of Normandy: A True Story of World War II Told Through Drawings by Children.* New York: Atheneum Books for Young Readers.
- Borden, Louise. (1997). *The Little Ships: The Heroic Rescue at Dunkirk in World War II.* New York: Margaret K. McElderry Books.
- McCann, Michelle R. (2003). *Luba: The Angel of Bergen-Belsen.* Berkley, CA: Tricycle Press.
- Mochizuki, Ken. (1977). *Passage to Freedom: The Sugihara Story.* New York: Lee & Low Books, Inc.
- Polacco, Patricia. (2000). *The Butterfly.* New York: Scholastic, Inc.
- Poole, Josephine. *(2005). Anne Frank.* New York: Alfred A. Knopf.
- Rubin, Susan Goldman. (2001). *Fireflies in the Dark: The Story of Friedl Dicker-Brandeis and the Children of Terezin.* New York: Scholastic, Inc.
- Russo, Marisabina. (2005). *Always Remember Me: How One Family Survived World War II.* New York: An Anne Schwartz Book.

### *Japanese-American Internment Camps*

- Bunting, Eve. (1998). *So Far from the Sea.* New York: Clarion Books.
- Noguchi, Rick and Jenks, Deneen. (2001). *Flowers from Mariko.* New York: Lee & Low Books, Inc.
- Say, Allen. (2002). *Home of the Brave.* Boston: Houghton Mifflin Company.
- Tunnell, Michael O. and Chilcoat, George W. (1996). *The Children of Topaz: The Story of a Japanese-American Internment Camp.* New York: Holiday House.

# Teaching Ideas—Lesson Plans and Extension/Application Activities

Tarry Lindquist's first book, *Seeing the Whole Through Social Studies,* describes how she integrates all of her fifth-grade curriculum except math using the social studies themes/content as the organizing framework. Her second book, *Ways That Work: Putting Social Studies Standards into Practice* models how the National Social Studies standards are easily met through local curriculum. Both of Lindquist's books contain wonderful teaching strategies that actively engage students in the study of social studies. Although she is writing about fifth grade, most of her ideas and strategies can be adapted or adopted for younger students.

One of Lindquist's techniques for gathering data is the Data Disk. Together, she and her students determine what categories of data they will gather about a given subject. In *Seeing the Whole* her students are each responsible for gathering data about early explorers to North America. This format has the following advantages: data to be gathered are focused; data are gathered in notes not sentences; and the data disk can be a final product (like Report in a Can in Chapter 3) or a data-gathering device. In the following lesson, students engage in two activities using the data disks during a "jigsaw lesson." First students gather data about explorers, then report their findings about the explorers to other students. Allow two lessons for this activity so that students arc not rushed.

## *Lesson Plan 4.1—Exploring Explorers*

### LEVEL: GRADE 2 (WITH TEACHER SUPPORT OR OLDER STUDENT "BUDDIES"); GRADES 3 AND 4

### Learning Goals

- Students will gather and organize data about explorers.
- Students will share the data with other students.
- Students will compare and contrast the explorers.

### Assessment

- Formal assessment (individual student): Data disk.

    +3   Data disk contains accurate details in all categories
         Student can discuss data with ease
    +2   Data disk contains details in all categories
         Student can discuss data with prompting
    +1   Data disk has missing or inaccurate information
         Student struggles with discussion from data

- Formal Assessment (small group): Attribute chart with timeline.

    +3   Attribute chart is well organized and complete with accurate data
         Students can compare and contrast information with ease
    +2   Attribute chart shows organization and is complete
         Students can compare and contrast information with prompting
    +1   Attribute chart is disorganized and/or has missing or inaccurate data
         Students struggle with discussion from data

### Materials

- Explorer Data Disks: one per student (Some students may need a larger data disk or lines drawn in the disk cells.)
- Explorer Data Disk overhead transparency
- Attribute Chart and Timeline worksheet: one per "home" group
- Attribute Chart and Timeline overhead transparency
- Informational books about explorers (based on the curricular requirements)

### Key Questions and/or Vocabulary

   Note: Use the following questions or formulate others to meet curricular needs:

- What is the focus of the exploration?
- What is the significance of the exploration?
- What country/government did the explorer represent?
- What are the dates of the explorer's birth/death and explorations?

## Procedure

### Motivation and Explanation

- Tell students that they are going to be experts today. They will be gathering information about six explorers—one for each expert group to research.
- Divide the class into small groups. Use this organizational framework:
  If there are 24 students to study six explorers, first create four "home" groups with six students in each. Within each group, have the students count off from 1 to 6. Each student will represent the home group in an expert group—one for each of the explorers. Home groups have six members; expert groups have four members. Although the number of students and the number of explorers may vary, the organization of the groups is the same (See Figure 4.1).

### Table of Home Groups and Expert Groups

| Home group #1 Ann, Beth, Carl, Dave, Ethan, Fran | | Home group #2 Adam, Ben, Carol, Diane, Edie, Fred | | Home group #3 Alicia, Betsy, Clara, Dot, Ella, Felicity | | Home group #4 Aaron, Bob, Candy, Dan, Elise, Flora |
|---|---|---|---|---|---|---|
| Expert #1 Ann, Adam, Alicia, Aaron | Expert #2 Beth, Ben, Betsy, Bob | Expert #3 Carl, Carol, Clara, Candy | Expert #4 Dave, Diane, Dot, Dan | Expert #5 Ethan, Edie, Ella, Elise | Expert #6 Fran, Fred, Felicity, Flora |

**Figure 4.1** Table of home groups and expert groups.

### Demonstration and Modeling

- Display the Explorer Data Disk using an overhead transparency and projector.
- Read the four categories for data collection found in the data disk cells. This is the data-gathering device each person will fill out during the expert group activity.
- Read an informational book aloud to the class and "think aloud" about information read; determine where one or two items fit on the data disk. Use phrases and words, not sentences.
- Tell students that they need to know what the phrases and words mean because they will teach members of their home group after the expert groups have gathered data.

### Guided Practice

- Read further and ask students to let you know when there is information that should be added to the data disk.
- Display the Attribute Chart and Timeline on the overhead projector. Ask students to help transfer information just gathered on the data disk to the Attribute Chart and Timeline. Note that because your example is the only one on the Attribute Chart and Timeline you do not need to be concerned with the order of the dates. When the

home groups meet, however, they should place the explorers on the chart in the order of their explorations, beginning with the earliest.

### Independent Practice

- Organize students first as home groups; while in this grouping, they should determine which students will be in the expert groups. Send students to the expert groups with appropriate materials, for example, data disks and informational books.
- Support students' data-gathering as you circulate among the groups.
- Send students back to home groups when all groups have completed the data disks.
- Have the students in the home groups create a timeline with the data disks. Once they have determined the earliest to the most recent explorers, the earliest expert should then begin to share the information on the data disk with the rest of the home group. Place this data on the Attribute Chart and Timeline. (This home activity may need to take place during the next class because of time constraints or students' attention spans.)

### Closure/Reflection

- Use the Attribute Chart and Timeline overhead transparency to gather data about all of the explorers.
- Ask students to compare and contrast the information. Prepare questions based on the information students should know about the specific explorers and general information about exploration to direct this closing discussion. For example, ask "Who explored for the same country? Who explored in the same time period? Who explored the same places? Who explored for the same reasons?"

Hands-on experiences are vital to university students who are learning to teach in elementary classrooms. Each semester students in one social studies class go to the Stroud Mansion that houses the Monroe County Historical Association (MCHA). Kathy Boyle, a retired K–12 social studies supervisor, has been actively involved in the MCHA's work for many years. Students are divided into two groups. Kathy and the MCHA's director, Amy Leiser, each take a group for half the time. Kathy provides a primary sources workshop and Amy provides an informational tour of the Stroud Mansion.

During the workshop, students engage in two or three lessons that align with state history and geography standards and use primary sources available at the Mansion via MCHA. Kathy demonstrates to the students the connections to and ease of integration with other curricular requirements for elementary-grade students. University students are encouraged to use the lessons in their elementary classroom placements and to share them with their mentor teachers.

The following lesson using the 1880 Census for Stroudsburg, Pennsylvania, meets a number of state standards:

### History (PA Standard 4)

- The student engages in historical analysis and interpretation..
- The student conducts historical research.

### English Languages Arts (PA Standard 7)

- Students conduct research on issues and interests by generating ideas and questions, and by posing problems. They gather, evaluate, and synthesize data from a variety of sources (e.g., print and nonprint, artifacts, people) to communicate their discoveries in ways that suit their purpose and audience.

### Economics (PA Standard 1)

- Productive resources are limited. Therefore people cannot have all the goods and services they want; as a result, they must choose some things and give up others.

### Mathematics—Data Analysis and Probability Standard for Grades 3, 4, and 5

*Anchor—Grade 3 PSSA*

- Formulate questions that can be addressed with data and collect, organize, and display relevant data to answer them.
- Select and use appropriate statistical methods to analyze data.
- Develop and evaluate inferences and predictions that are based on data.

  This lesson addresses elements of Geography Standards 11 and 12.

## *Lesson Plan 4.2—Uncovering Patterns*

### LEVEL: GRADES 3 AND 4

### Learning Goals

- Students will analyze (identify and categorize) information in the census.
- Students will synthesize information in the census.
- Students will create a bar graph.

### Assessment

- Informal Assessment: Observation of discussion about census uses and content found in census materials.
- Informal Assessment: Graph created by class.

### Materials

- Paper copy of pages (from microfilm) of 1880 Census for Stroudsburg. The pages in the packet give a representative sampling of the Stroudsburg population.
  Locate census data for the county in which you teach. Most communities have historical associations to contact, or check with the local county government.
- Transcription of name, age, relationship, occupation, and place of birth columns of the preceding census page.
- Large piece of graph paper.
- Overhead transparency of one page of transcription
- Patterns of Occupation bar graph worksheet
- Patterns of Occupation bar graph overhead transparency

### Key Questions and/or Vocabulary

- census
- population
- occupation

### Procedure

#### *Motivation and Explanation*

Ask students how information about people in the country (census) is gathered. Also ask, "How often does this happen? What would be the purpose in gathering information? What might be useful information? and How could the information be used at the time it is gathered and years later?"

#### *Demonstration and Modeling*

- Show the transparency of the microfilm copy of census page and explain what a census is. Note that the information is hand written but the copies that students will receive is typed so that they are easier to read.

- Discuss column headings of the 1880 census.
- Focus on the occupation column.
- Ask students to identify occupations that appear unfamiliar to them. Point out that they will have an opportunity to find out what type of work these people did.
- Ask students if there are other ways of displaying the occupation information. Suggest that it would be nice to get a quick idea of the numbers of people who did each job.

### Guided Practice

- Distribute one page of transcription of 1880 census to student pairs.
- This activity requires students to complete a tally and create a simple bar graph. *This task should be a reinforcement of what has been taught and practiced in math.*

  - Ask students to create a list of occupations on their page.
  - Have them tally the number of people engaged in each of those occupations.
  - Allow students to use the Patterns of Occupations bar graph worksheet to graph the occupations based on their tally. Monitor students' progress and assist where necessary
  - Ask students if they think their census page gives a good idea of how people earned a living in Stroudsburg in 1880. Discuss their responses and provide suggestions for how to obtain a better picture.
  - Students should say something like, "Let's combine our information."

- Display a large bar graph or use an overhead transparency of the Patterns of Occupations bar graph.
- Have students share the occupations found on their page, and list on the class bar graph.
- Record each pair's contribution and ask the class for the total.
- Fill in the graph column with the total. Explain the process.
- Do another example if students need additional practice. Otherwise, total the remaining occupations and invite students to fill in the appropriate bar.

### Closure/Reflection

- Ask what occupation(s) appears most frequently. Consider possible reasons.
- Ask what occupation(s) appears the least frequently. Consider possible reasons.
- Ask if there are occupations that are rare or that no longer exist today.
- Review the difference between goods and services. Have students give their definitions rather than simply giving the information to them; state examples of goods and services if needed.
- Ask what occupation provides a service for the community.
- Ask what occupations provide goods in the community.
- Ask students, "Based on what you see on the graph, do you think that Stroudsburg is a growing community?"
- Review the census page. Ask who seems to be doing most of the work outside the home, men or women?

- Ask students what conclusions they can draw about the occupations of women? Are there any exceptions? Ask what explanations they can provide for their answers.
- Ask what job on the graph students would like to do and why?

## Extension/Application Activity 4.1—Researching Occupations

### LEVEL: GRADES 3 AND 4

These activities can follow the lesson. They might be part of another lesson or independent work that students complete at a center or in a research assignment.

**Research occupations that are not well known to students.**

- Write a job description for the occupation. List the skills the applicant needs to make the goods or to provide the service.
- Write an ad for the place of business. Examine late 1800s ads and create an ad that reflects the time period.
- Use maps and photos from the time period to facilitate discussion.
- Discuss occupations that are unique to the area because of its geography.

## Lesson Plan 4.3—"Little House"

### LEVEL: KINDERGARTEN AND GRADE 1 (WHOLE GROUP TIMELINE ACTIVITY) GRADES 2 AND 3

### Learning Goals

• Students will compare and contrast urban, suburban, and rural settings.
• Students will show change over time.

### Assessment

• Informal Assessment: Observation of discussion about changes in the setting and characteristics of urban, suburban, and rural during read-aloud.
• Formal Assessment: Timeline.

    ✓+  Timeline shows changes in the Little House's life and the student can explain the pictures using rural, suburban, and urban.

    ✓  Timeline shows changes in the Little House's life and student can explain using rural, suburban, and urban with prompting.

    ✓–  Timeline has errors and student cannot explain rural, suburban, and urban.

### Materials

• *The Little House* by Virginia Lee Burton
• two strips of white construction paper (4 × 12-inch) for each student
• transparent tape

### Key Questions and/or Vocabulary

• urban: city or town (opposite of rural)
• suburban: residential area lying just outside a city or town
• rural: an area made up of farmland or countryside (opposite of urban)
• timeline: a visual way to organize events or changes over time

### Procedure

#### Motivation and Explanation

• Display the book, *The Little House,* and ask students what they think the story will be about, and where they think it takes place and why.
• Read the book, showing the illustrations. Make the read-aloud interactive by asking questions to guide thinking. Stop along the way as significant events are about to take place in the story. Use "think-pair-share" to give everyone a chance to share ideas, even if it is with only one student. Encourage the students to predict what will happen next.
• Ask students to think back to their first predictions about what the story would be about and where it takes place. (Lead students to point out that the environment/place changed.)

### Demonstration and Modeling

- Tell students that the little house and its environment changed over time. It started out as a house in the country and ended there. The term for being in the country is *rural*.
- Tell students that they could show the changes and moves in the little house's life by creating a timeline. A timeline is a visual way to organize events or changes over time.

### Guided Practice

- Ask students to think back to the parts of the story when the house was not in the country.
- Ask the students to describe those times, and be sure to use the terms *suburban* and *urban* and define them. As students recall parts of the story and how the environment changed, show them illustrations in the book that show the changes.
- Discuss where students live and whether they have visited or lived in any or all of the three designated environments.
- Show students two strips of construction paper. Fold each strip in thirds to create sections that are 4 × 4 inches. Tape the two strips together. Draw a picture of the Little House in the country in the first section. Ask students where the Little House should be in the last section (the country). Draw a picture of the Little House in the country in the last section. Ask them, "What is the term we are using for country?" They should respond "rural."

### Independent Practice

- Give each student two strips of construction paper. Have students draw the Little House in the country in the first section of the first strip and again on the last section of the second strip.
- Students should now draw what happened to the Little House and its environment as it changed from rural to suburban to urban.

### Closure/Reflection

- Ask students to share their images with the class using rural, suburban, and rural.
- Ask students to explain the purpose of a timeline

# Review Game—Footloose

## LEVEL: GRADES 2, 3, AND 4

This is a wonderful review game that can be used with any subject. The Footloose game board included at the end of the chapter has spaces for 25 answers, but vary the number of questions/answers in your review.

### Preparing Footloose

- Determine what you want students to know.
- Create as many questions as you want. Have at least as many questions as students in your class.

- Consider how much time it will take students to answer each question. The time should be very similar; try to stay within ½- to 1-minute time frame.
- Be sure the answer will fit into the box on the Footloose game board.

- Number the questions and transfer them to 3 × 5-inch or 4 × 6-inch index cards. Consider using the label function in the Microsoft Word program. That ensures legible print for the labels.
- Write the number of the question on the back of the card. Laminating the cards will give them a longer game life.

## Playing Footloose

- Duplicate as many game board sheets as needed.
- Distribute the cards around the room in numerical order, placing one card on each student's desk with the back of the card (with the number) showing.

  - If there are more cards than students, place the extra ones on other surfaces in numerical order.

- Give each student a Footloose game board and a pencil.
- Have each student begin at his desk and answer that question card first. Then move to the desk with the card for the next number.
- Clearly explain the pattern of movement. If there are cards on surfaces other than students' desks, students need to know what the numbers are and where to move next.
- Tell students you will say "begin." At that time everyone should read and answer the question in the right box on their game board. Check to be sure everyone is in the correct spot before proceeding.
- Have students turn the card upside down when answered. When it appears that everyone has finished (or 1 minute has elapsed), say "move," and students can go to the next card.
- Continue until all cards are answered.
- Have students read the cards (in order) and answer the questions to finish the game. Make sure students correct their own game board. Be sure to clarify any misconceptions that appear when answers are shared. The incorrect answers most likely represent the concepts students need to study. The Footloose game sheet becomes a review sheet to carry home.

## Alternative Playing Format

For this format to work, you must have three to five question cards more than students.

- Distribute the cards around the room as before.
- Students begin at their own desk, but may move at their own pace and answer cards in any order.
- Preset a reasonable time for play. Provide a time warning at about halfway and again five and two minutes from the end of the game time.

# References

Lindquist, Tarry. (1995). *Seeing the Whole Through Social Studies.* Portsmouth, NH: Heinemann

Lindquist, Tarry. (1997). *Ways That Work: Putting Social Studies Standards into Practice.* Portsmouth, NH: Heinemann.

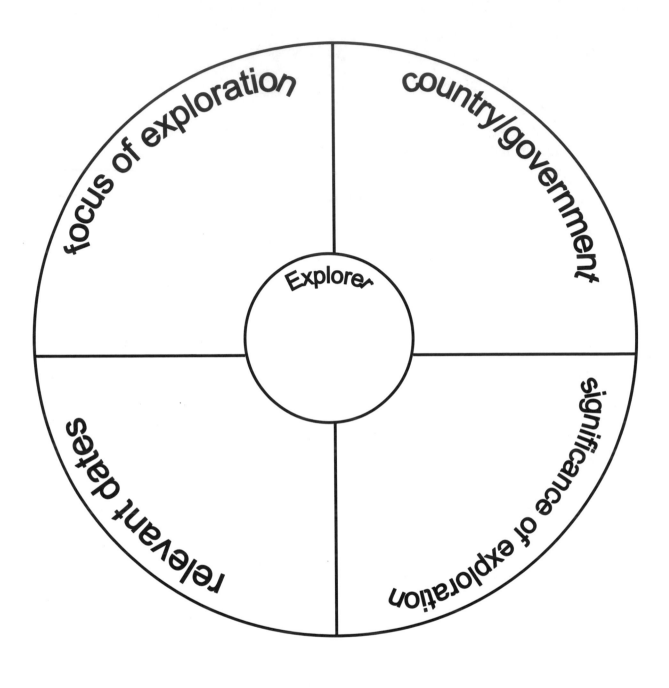

focus of exploration

country/government

Explorer

significance of exploration

relevant dates

## Attribute Chart and Timeline

List the explorers in the order of their exploration years. Then identify the other important information about the explorers.

| Explorer's Name | Relevant Dates | Country/Government Representing | Focus of Exploration | Significance of Exploration |
|---|---|---|---|---|
| | | | | |
| | | | | |
| | | | | |
| | | | | |
| | | | | |

Be prepared to answer these questions: Who explored during the same time in history? Do you think the explorers were successful? Why or why not? Whose explorations were most important and—why? How did these explorations affect our country or the world?

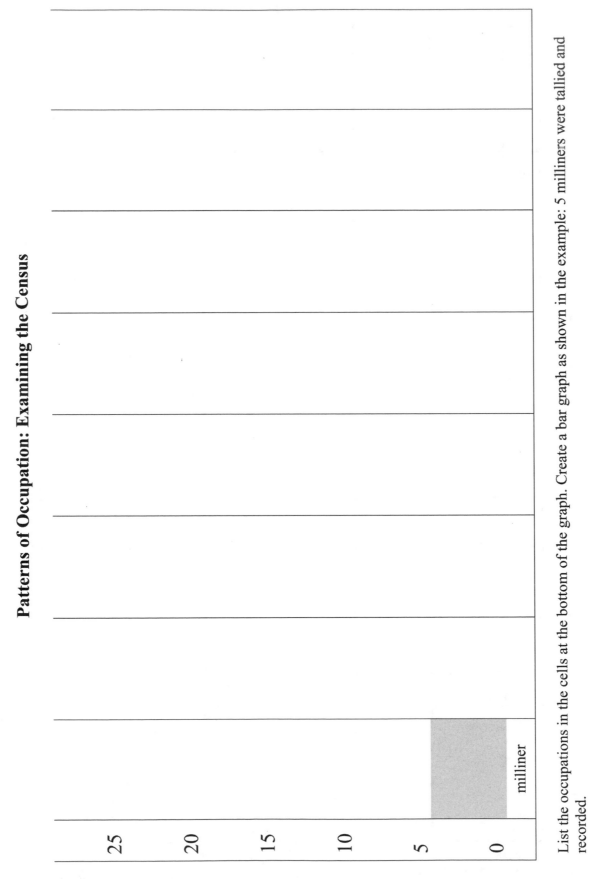

**Patterns of Occupation: Examining the Census**

| | | | | | | | |
|---|---|---|---|---|---|---|---|
| 25 | | | | | | | |
| 20 | | | | | | | |
| 15 | | | | | | | |
| 10 | | | | | | | |
| 5 | | | | | | | |
| 0 | | | | | | | milliner |

List the occupations in the cells at the bottom of the graph. Create a bar graph as shown in the example: 5 milliners were tallied and recorded.

# FOOTLOOSE

| | | | | |
|---|---|---|---|---|
| 1 | 2 | 3 | 4 | 5 |
| 6 | 7 | 8 | 9 | 10 |
| 11 | 12 | 13 | 14 | 15 |
| 16 | 17 | 18 | 19 | 20 |
| 21 | 22 | 23 | 24 | 25 |

## CHAPTER 5

# Environment and Society

Physical and human phenomena are spatially distributed over Earth's surface. The outcome of *Geography for Life* is a geographically informed person (1) who sees meaning in the arrangement of things in space; (2) who sees relations between people, places, and environments; (3) who uses geographic skills; and (4) who applies spatial and ecological perspectives to life situations.

## ENVIRONMENT AND SOCIETY

The physical environment is modified by human activities, largely as a consequence of the ways in which human societies value and use Earth's natural resources, and human activities are also influenced by Earth's physical features and processes.

The geographically informed person knows and understands:

14. How human actions modify the physical environment.
    a. How people depend on the physical environment.
    b. How people modify the physical environment.
    c. That the physical environment can both accommodate and be endangered by human activities.

15. How physical systems affect human systems.
    a. How variations within the physical environment produce spatial patterns that affect human adaptation.
    b. The ways in which the physical environment provides opportunities for people.
    c. The ways in which the physical environment constrains human activities.

16. The changes that occur in the meaning, use, distribution, and importance of resources.
    a. The characteristics of renewable, nonrenewable, and flow resources.
    b. The spatial distribution of resources.
    c. The role of resources in daily life.

*Geography for Life: National Geography Standards* (National Council for the Social Studies, 1994, pp. 35, 132–138).

The standards within Environment and Society address how humans interact with the environment in three general ways: how humans modify the physical environment, how physical systems affect human systems, and issues related to natural resources. Attention to these issues is now at a higher level than in the past. For example, third-grade science content in the state of Virginia's curriculum includes renewable and nonrenewable resources, as well as how humans can protect both. This Essential Element reflects the theme Relationships within Places: Humans and Environments. This is such an important area of learning for students because their understanding of the concepts and all the implications will affect their future.

## Text Sets—Human/Environmental Interaction, Climate/Weather, Construction/Architecture

The books in this chapter are divided into three text sets: Human-Environmental Interaction, Climate/Weather, and Construction/Architecture. The first set is rather large and looks at both the positive and negative aspects of the relationship for both humans and Earth.

### Human/Environmental Interaction

As the Human/Environmental Interaction text set was organized, it was noted that the issue of natural resources (addressed in Standard 16) was subtly included in many of the books or in an author's end notes. *Recycle!: A Handbook for Kids,* however, is not subtle and is another example of how beautifully Gail Gibbons provides rich in-depth content in a student-friendly format.

*Brother Eagle, Sister Sky* and *John Muir, America's First Environmentalist* are lovely books. Guiberson's three books, Johnston's *Desert Song,* and Siebert's *Cave* all point out the fragile balance of nature and our ability and need to make sure it remains in balance. Jeannie Baker, an Australian author, once again tells a beautiful visual story of how humans can restore poorly cared for areas to health. Cherry's *The Great Kapok Tree* and *A River Ran Wild* join in the plea to care for the earth.

In *Color for Thought,* fifth graders share the natural sources of the colors people use and enjoy in life from clothes to food. Cherry's *The Shaman's Apprentice* shows how the environment—the rain forest in particular—holds answers to health concerns. Fleischman's fantasy, *Weslandia,* illustrates how the environment provides for human needs.

### Human/Environmental Interaction

- Baker, Jeannie. (2004). *Home.* New York: Greenwillow Books.
- Cherry, Lynne. (1992). *A River Ran Wild.* San Diego: A Gulliver Green Book.
- Cherry, Lynne. (2000). *The Great Kapok Tree: A Tale of the Amazon Rain Forest.* San Diego: Voyager Books Harcourt, Inc.
- Cherry, Lynne, and Plotkin, Mark J. (1998). *The Shaman's Apprentice: A Tale of the Amazon Rain Forest.* San Diego: A Gulliver Green Book.
- Fifth-grade Students of Coast Episcopal School. (2004). *Color for Thought.* New York: Scholastic.
- Fleischman, Paul. (2000). *Weslandia.* New York: Scholastic, Inc.
- Gibbons, Gail. (1992). *Recycle!: A Handbook for Kids.* Boston: Little, Brown and Company.

- Guiberson, Brenda Z. (1992). *Spoonbill Swamp.* New York: Henry Holt and Company.
- Guiberson, Brenda Z. (1995). *Winter Wheat.* New York: Henry Holt and Company.
- Guiberson, Brenda Z. (1998). *Cactus Hotel.* New York: Scholastic, Inc.
- Jeffers, Susan. (1991). *Brother Eagle, Sister Sky: A Message for Chief Seattle.* New York: Dial Books.
- Johnston, Tony. (2000). *Desert Song.* San Francisco: Sierra Club Books for Children.
- Lasky, Kathryn. (2006). *John Muir: America's First Environmentalist.* Cambridge, MA: Candlewick Press.
- Siebert, Diane. (2000). *Cave.* New York: HarperCollins Publishers.

## *Climate/Weather*

The five books in the Climate/Weather text set could be included in the Human-Environmental Interactions, but they are separate here because time is spent in the primary grades checking the daily weather and discussing its influence on how students dressed for the day. Climate—long-term weather and precipitation trends—influences more than what people wear. Homes are built of materials that withstand the yearly effect of the climate. Climate also shapes part of the economy for a community or region. The crops grown, the businesses operated, and the recreational activities that people enjoy are also influenced by the climate.

The dramatic story in *Togo* tells how residents in the Arctic used dogsleds to traverse difficult terrain in extreme weather. *The Blizzard* is a delightful story of a winter birthday celebration changed by an unexpected storm, while *City of Snow* relates the story of a historic snow fall in New York City that had a long-term impact on the city. Like the Great Chicago Fire, the Great Blizzard of March 1888 brought about changes in the city's infrastructure that continue to influence cities today. Lyon's and Wallner's stories both demonstrate the effect weather has on people's lives.

### Climate/Weather

- Blake, Robert. (2002). *Togo.* New York: Philomel Books.
- High, Linda Oatman. (2004). *City of Snow.* New York: Walker and Company.
- Lyon, George Ella. (2000). *One Lucky Girl.* New York: Dorling Kindersley Publishing, Inc.
- Wallner, Alexandra. (2000). *Sergio and the Hurricane.* New York: Henry Holt and Company.
- Wright, Betty Ren. (2003). *The Blizzard.* New York: Holiday House.

## *Construction/Architecture*

There are some lovely books in the Construction/Architecture set that show how cleverly humans have learned to shape the land or build remarkable structures despite the land formation. *Arches to Zigzags* and *B Is for Bulldozer* are two alphabet books that will delight many readers. Harness shares the story of the Erie Canal construction in the early 1800s with rich illustrations and informative diagrams. This remarkable human feat connected the Great Lakes to the Hudson River and opened trade routes to the interior of the country.

Within this set are some great pairs. *Pop's Bridge* tells the story of the Golden Gate Bridge's construction through the eyes of a fictional boy. Sturges includes the Golden Gate among the bridges around the world, using brief informational paragraphs and incredible collage illustrations. Hopkinson and Mann both tell the construction story of the Empire State Building. Hopkinson's fictional and Mann's factual accounts are perfect complements, as are High's simple *Under New York* and Kent's complex *Hidden Under the Ground*.

### Construction/Architecture

- Bunting, Eve. (2006). *Pop's Bridge*. Orlando: Harcourt, Inc.
- Crosbie, Michael J., Rosenthal, Steve and Rosenthal, Kit. (2000). *Arches to Zigzags: An Architecture ABC*. New York: Harry N. Abrams, Inc.
- Harness, Cheryl. (1999). *The Amazing Impossible Erie Canal*. New York: Aladdin Paperbacks.
- High, Linda Oatman. (2001). *Under New York*. New York: Holiday House.
- Hopkinson, Deborah. (2006). *Sky Boys: How They Built the Empire State Building*. New York: Schwartz and Wade Books.
- Kent, Peter. (1998). *Hidden Under the Ground: The World Beneath Your Feet*. New York: Dutton Children's Books.
- Mann, Elizabeth. (2003). *Empire State Building*. New York: Mikaya Press.
- Sobel, June. (2003). *B Is for Bulldozer: A Construction ABC*. San Diego: Gulliver Books.
- Sturges, Philemon. (1998). *Bridges are to Cross*. New York: G. P. Putnam's Sons.

## Teaching Ideas—Lesson Plans and Extension/Application Activities

The following is an introductory lesson based on third-grade curriculum requirements in a local school district that engages students in a unit about goods and services in the community. A basic concept of this unit is the way in which humans meet the four basic needs. This concept and the difference between wants and needs are introduced in kindergarten and revisited each year. The *Weslandia* lesson examines how people meet their basic needs. Unlike Wesley, people depend on others in the community who provide goods and services that assist in meeting needs and acquiring wants.

## Lesson Plan 5.1—Meeting Our Needs

LEVEL: GRADES 2, 3 AND 4

### Learning Goals

- Students will describe how Wesley met his four basic needs in *Weslandia*.
- Students will compare how their needs are met with how Wesley met his needs.

### Assessment

- Informal Assessment: Teacher observation of discussion
- Formal Assessment: Graphic Organizer

  - Graphic organizer: Rubric
  - +3  graphic organizer is fully completed with appropriate responses and details
  - +2  graphic organizer is completed with appropriate responses, no details
  - +1  graphic organizer has missing or inappropriate responses, no details

### Materials

- *Weslandia* by Paul Fleishman (multiple copies, if possible)
- *Weslandia* graphic organizer
- *Weslandia* graphic organizer overhead transparency

### Key Questions and/or Vocabulary

- What are the four basic needs that all humans have? (food, shelter, clothing, love).
- How do people meet these needs?
- Does meeting needs vary from place to place?
- What is the difference between wants and needs?

### Procedure

*Motivation and Explanation*

- Say to students: "I was thinking about an advertisement I heard this morning on the radio. The announcer said, 'Everyone *needs* the new Verizon wireless phone!' But, I do not think everyone *needs* a phone. What do you think?"
- Lead the students in a discussion that discriminates between needs and wants. If such discussion does not occur spontaneously, introduce the idea of participating in the TV program *Survivor.* Ask students what the people on the program need to survive.
- Show students the cover of the book, *Weslandia,* and ask what they think the book is about.
- Divide students into five groups (or as many as you have books to share). Tell them they are to read the story together and consider this question: "What connection do you think there might be between this book and the class discussion about wants and needs?" NOTE: This book can be read independently by third- and

fourth-grade students. If using it with younger students, engage in a read-aloud as a whole class.

- Give students time to read as you circulate to monitor their progress.
- Ask again, "What connection do you think there might be between this book and the class discussion about wants and needs?" when students finish reading the book.

### Demonstration and Modeling

- Place the graphic organizer on the overhead projector. Tell students they are going to compare the way Wesley met his needs with the way their families meet their needs.
- Think aloud, saying, "My family grocery shops every week, and in the summer has a small garden." Write grocery store and garden in the Food section under US.

### Guided Practice

- Ask students to think about the story. Ask what Wesley did to meet his needs. Record one or two answers in the correct box.

### Independent Practice

- Distribute the graphic organizer handout and tell students they are to record information about how the people in their groups meet the needs in the organizer, as well as how Wesley met his needs.

### Closure/Reflection

- Have students contribute their answers as you write them in the organizer on the overhead transparency.
- Ask students to compare methods for meeting needs today to Wesley's methods.
- Ask students why people around the world might meet their needs in ways that are different from theirs. Consider the physical features and economic conditions in other locations as part of the discussion.
- Discuss the difference between wants and needs.

*A River Ran Wild* by Lynne Cherry is the fictionalized story of the polluting and clean-up of the Nashua River in Massachusetts. It is a beautiful book that can be used for two different lessons. The first lesson is an altered version of a lesson created by Anne B. Miller. Anne combined the Fred the Fish activity found in *Geographic Literacy Through Children's Literature* with *A River Ran Wild*. Fred the Fish was adapted from "A Fish Story" designed by Pat Chilton for Michigan's Kalamazoo Soil Conservation District in July 1979. It is a scripted adventure set in an imaginary river. Anne used the elements from that activity and applied it to the true story of the polluting of the Nashua River as told by Lynne Cherry.

The closing activity in the "A Fish Story" simulation has students brainstorm ways to clean up the river. One teacher used "A Fish Story" activity during her third-grade science lesson one day. The next day she and the students created a filtering system and ran the polluted water through the filter to demonstrate how water is purified for our use.

## *Lesson Plan 5.2—Polluting a River*

### LEVEL: KINDERGARTEN AND GRADE 1(WITH WHOLE GROUP TIMELINE), GRADES 2, 3, AND 4

### Learning Goals

- Students will observe and record changes in the river.
- Students will describe how Chief Weeawa may have felt about the changes in the river.
- Students will identify causes of pollution.

### Assessment

- Informal Assessment: Observation of students' responses during discussion and students' responses on the river timeline.

### Materials

- *A River Ran Wild* by Lynne Cherry
  Note: This lesson requires specific stopping places along the way so that the river can be "polluted" with materials that represent the action in the story. A suggestion is to use Post-it notes with directions for the teacher about which cups to empty and what the materials represent. Also, students do not respond at every stop, so note that as well.
- Large map of United States
- Nashua River Timeline handout (1 per student)
- Nashua River Timeline overhead transparency (optional)
- Large clear plastic tub filled half full with clean water (or large clear glass or plastic jar; two-gallon capacity is best for all to be able to see the activity)
- Plastic cups or small containers filled as identified next. Number and fill cups with ingredients as follows:

| | |
|---|---|
| #1 pebbles | #6 green food coloring container |
| #2 toothpicks or twigs | #7 sawdust or mulch (or pencil shavings) |
| #3 yarn clippings | #8 blue food coloring |
| #4 red food coloring container | #9 yellow food coloring container |
| #5 punched construction paper dots | |

### Key Questions and/or Vocabulary

- pollution: the direct or indirect process resulting from human action by which part of the environment is made potentially or actually unhealthy
- environment: anything in or on Earth's surface and it's atmosphere

### Procedure

#### *Motivation and Explanation*

- Say, "Today we're going to read a story that tells the environmental history of a river in Massachusetts called the Nashua River."

- Find the Nashua River on the U.S. map.
- Say, "Think about what this area might have looked like thousands of years ago, before settlers came from Europe. Think about what we know about Native Americans."
- Show students the maps on the endpapers of the book that show New England in the 1500s and 1900s. Discuss the changes.

### *Demonstration and Modeling*

- Show students the overhead transparency of the Nashua River Timeline. Tell students that another way to show changes is to use a timeline that puts events in the order they occur.

### *Guided Practice*

- Position the "river" in the center of the classroom so that everyone has a clear view.
- Distribute the Nashua River Timelines to the students and place cups around the room so that students can empty the contents at the appropriate point.
- Remind students to note the number on the cup but not to touch it until it is time to use it.
- Say, "We will stop from time to time and record our thoughts or observations on the timeline. As a class, we are going to bring the story to life as we recreate the river and what happens to it."
- Tell students to empty the contents of the containers into the "river" (tub/jar) when their cup's number is called. All students should then record on their timelines as prompted.
- Begin reading the text: "Long ago . . . "
- Read page 5. Empty cup number one into the river.
- Say, "Record on your timeline how the river looks and how Chief Weeawa might feel about the river." Have students identify what is being emptied into the river. Note: Ask a few students to share what they have written on the timeline. If the students are first- or second-graders, ask for responses first, then record them on the overhead. Then students can either select one from the choices or their own. Recording will be a challenge for some young students.
- Follow the same pattern with participation as follows:

| | |
|---|---|
| Read page 11. Empty cup number two. | Record on sheet. (settlers' logs) |
| Read page 15. Empty cups three and four. | Record on sheet. (industrial revolution) |
| Read page 18. Empty cups five and six. | Do not record. (age of plastics) |
| Read page 19. Empty cups seven, eight, and nine. | Record on sheets. (chemicals) |
| Read page 27. | Ask, "How might Chief Weeawa feel about the river now?" (clean-up) |

### *Independent Practice*

- Have students work with a partner to determine why they think the river became so polluted. They can record this information on the back of the timeline sheet.

### *Closure/Reflection*

- Share students' responses.

## *Extension/Application Activity 5.1*

### LEVEL: GRADES 3 AND 4

- Read *Home* by Jeannie Baker. This story about the change in an urban neighborhood from neglected and unproductive to clean, attractive, and dynamic may be a more concrete example of how students can impact their environment.
- Encourage students to find a story of reclamation/rebirth in their own community. Invite someone involved in the reclamation to be a guest speaker for the class, or take students on a fieldtrip to the site.
- Establish a project for students to participate in that will impact the school or larger community (for example, a neighborhood park). See Documenting Changes at the end of the chapter for a way to document the project's success.

## *Lesson Plan 5.3—Caring for the Environment*

LEVEL: GRADES 2, 3, AND 4

### Learning Goals

- Students will compare and contrast how the Nashua Indians and the Europeans interacted with the Nashua River Valley.

### Assessment

- Informal Assessment: Observation of student responses in discussion.
- Formal Assessment: Venn diagram.

  Checklist: Venn diagram must be labeled correctly
  Minimum of three appropriate items in each area (differences and likenesses)

### Materials

- *A River Ran Wild* by Lynne Cherry
- Europeans and Native Americans Venn diagram worksheets (one for each pair of students)
- Europeans and Native Americans Venn diagram worksheet transparency

### Key Questions and/or Vocabulary

- environment—everything in and on Earth's surface and its atmosphere.
- cultural differences—differences in the learned behavior of people that include their belief systems, languages, material goods, etc.
- resources—aspects of the physical environment that people value and use to meet a need for fuel, food, or something else of value.
- conservation—preservation of the natural environment.

### Procedure

#### *Motivation and Explanation*

NOTE: This plan is written as a follow-up to Lesson 5.2. If it is used independently, which would also be effective, read the story with students in an interactive read-aloud format. Then proceed with the discussion and the picture walk.

- Gather students on the floor so they can all see the pictures easily.
- Say, "Think about what you did yesterday when this book was read." Show students the picture book, *A River Ran Wild.*
- Ask students to retell some of the things they learned during the lesson. Allow students to provide several facts. Note: Be sure to include a discussion of the conservative and descriptive use of the natural resources in the river and surrounding area.
- Say, "Let's take a picture walk through the book today looking for the actions of the Nashua Indians and the European settlers." Slowly move through the book and stop

to help students identify what is happening in the book. Pay particular attention to the thumbnail sketches around the text. Read the text if necessary to further explain what is happening in the story.

- Ask, "How did the Native Americans and the Europeans use the Nashua River and the land around it?"

### Demonstration and Modeling

- Have students return to their desks.
- Tell students that today they will use a Venn diagram to compare how the Native Americans and Europeans used the river and the land around it.
- Show the transparency of the Venn diagram on the overhead projector.
- Note that one circle is labeled "Europeans." In that circle, write the phrase: "fished in river."

### Guided Practice

- Pair students. Distribute a Venn diagram to each pair.
- Ask students to tell why the second circle is labeled "Native Americans" and the place where the two circles overlap is "Both."
- Ask students to look at the phrase written in the European circle. Is it placed correctly? Note: Because both the Europeans and Native Americans fished, it should be moved to the "Both" section.
- Ask students to provide something that shows only the Europeans' use of the river and land, then something that shows only the Native Americans' use of the river and the land. Record these on the overhead and have students record them on their Venn diagram.

### Independent Practice

- Say, "With your partner, think of at least two more things to put in each area of the Venn diagram."

### Closure/Reflection

- Have students share the information they wrote in their Venn diagrams. Write the additional information in the Venn diagram transparency. Encourage students to compare and contrast the effects of the actions.
- Students use only the knowledge gained from hearing the story for the purpose of this lesson. If this is part of a unit of study in which students have additional information, encourage them to include that information and to indicate the source.

## Documenting Changes—Somersault Book

### GRADES 2, 3, AND 4

If students decide to establish a clean-up project, consider using a Somersault Book format to document the changes. You may want to create one large class book or individual student books.

- Have students document the project with photographs, using a digital camera.
- In addition to visual records via the photos, have students record notes or keep a journal of the actions taken at each step in the clean-up project.
- Create the Somersault book when the project is complete. The format allows photos and word descriptions to be placed side by side. As it opens up and the pages unroll, the story is told in words and images. Note: The directions for the Somersault book appear at the end of this chapter. The format creates a final product that is relatively small. Change the proportions to meet the needs of your photos and written entries. Select a heavyweight paper or use poster board. Experiment with size and paper types before beginning the project. Note that the format on the directions shows the final product in a vertical format. Orient the photos and text to create a horizontal format if that displays the story more effectively.

# References

Rogers, Linda K. (1997). *Geographic Literacy Through Children's Literature.* Englewood, CO: Teacher Ideas Press.

# *Weslandia* Graphic Organizer

| US | ALL | WESLEY |
|---|---|---|
| | food | |
| | shelter | |
| | clothing | |
| | love | |

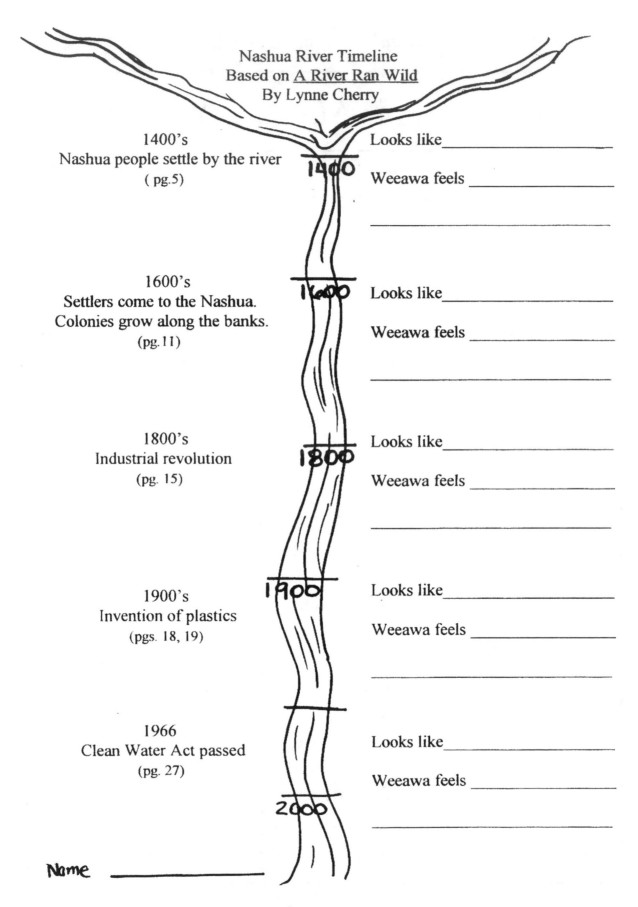

Nashua River Timeline
Based on <u>A River Ran Wild</u>
By Lynne Cherry

**1400's**
Nashua people settle by the river
( pg.5)

1400

Looks like_____

Weeawa feels _____

_____

**1600's**
Settlers come to the Nashua.
Colonies grow along the banks.
(pg.11)

1600

Looks like_____

Weeawa feels _____

_____

**1800's**
Industrial revolution
(pg. 15)

1800

Looks like_____

Weeawa feels _____

_____

**1900's**
Invention of plastics
(pgs. 18, 19)

1900

Looks like_____

Weeawa feels _____

_____

**1966**
Clean Water Act passed
(pg. 27)

Looks like_____

Weeawa feels _____

2000

_____

Name _____

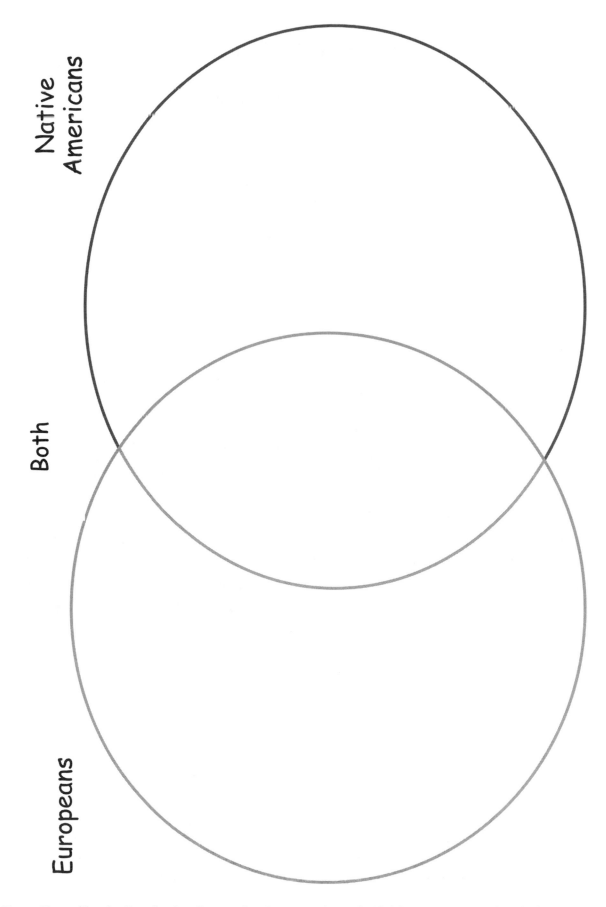

Native Americans

Both

Europeans

# Somersault Book

1. Cut a piece of heavy paper into a long rectangle of approximately 20" by 5". (Vary the proportions based on the size of the finished book you desire.)

2. Lay the piece of paper horizontally on a hard surface. Measure and mark 4 1/4" from the right end of the paper. Fold on that line, beginning to "somersault from the right to the left along the strip of paper.

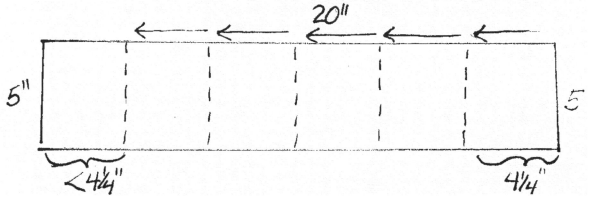

3. As you somersault be sure to place the leading edge firmly against the flat portion before you make the next fold. When you have finished you should have five almost equal sections and a sixth that is a bit less wide.

4. Place a brad in the center of the left side of the "cover" (last shorter section) about ½" from the fold. Glue a piece of ribbon or string across the front cover. Make sure the string is long enough to go around the book and loop around the head of the brad. Create a decorative cover sheet to hide the glued ribbon. When you close the book, wrap the ribbon around it and slide it around the brad to hold the book closed.

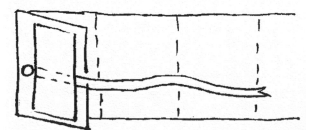

5. One way to use this book is to create pairs—one lined sheet of paper opposite a plain sheet of paper—that are related. For example, tell about the life cycle of an animal or plant. Provide both an illustration and a written description of the same stage. Or, identify the characters in a story. Provide an illustration and a written description of each character. Or...

## CHAPTER 6

# The Uses of Geography

Physical and human phenomena are spatially distributed over Earth's surface. The outcome of *Geography for Life* is a geographically informed person (1) who sees meaning in the arrangement of things in space; (2) who sees relations between people, places, and environments; (3) who uses geographic skills; and (4) who applies spatial and ecological perspectives to life situations.

**THE USES OF GEOGRAPHY**

Knowledge of geography enables people to develop an understanding of the relationships between people, places, and environments over time, that is, of Earth as it was, is, and might be.

The geographically informed person knows and understands:

17.  How to apply geography to interpret the past.
  a. How places and geographic contexts change over time.
  b. That people's perceptions of places and geographic contexts change over time.
  c. That geographic contexts influence people and events over time.

18.  How to apply geography to interpret the present and plan for the future.
  a. The dynamic character of geographic contexts.
  b. How people's perceptions affect their interpretations of the world.
  c. The spatial dimensions of social and environmental problems.

*Geography for Life: National Geography Standards* (National Council for the Social Studies, 1994, pp. 35, 139–141).

This sixth Essential Element recognizes the need for, and then encourages and demands, the geographically informed person to acknowledge and study the past, as well as plan for the future through the geographic lens. This suggests that the content of the previous five elements and the past be examined—the earth and its people—at the same time the present is interpreted; and in light of what is learned, plan for the future.

Archeological digs and attic discoveries offer ways to examine the recent and distant past. Artifacts and photographs serve as tools for uncovering information. These primary sources might be available in our own homes or in local historical associations. The

Library of Congress offers a wonderful Web site with primary sources and lesson plans for teachers (www.loc.gov/index.html) and (http://loc.gov/teachers/). The National Geographic Society's Web site is another rich classroom resource (www.nationalgeographic.com) and (www.nationalgeographic/xpeditions/lesson/indes.html).

## Text Sets—Other, Layers, Egypt

The books are organized into three text sets: Layers, Egypt, and Other. Layers and Egypt are related to Standard 17. The two books in Other point to the future. The text set discussion begins with that set. An excellent book for curriculum planning is *Understanding by Design* by Wiggins and McTighe. Its approach to curriculum planning begins with what the teacher wants students to know and be able to do at the end of the unit (or lesson)—designing backward. To assist students in planning for the future, determine how they can demonstrate that ability. The two books in the Other category offer models for how students might show planning for the future.

### *Other*

Elementary students and their teachers are invited to submit a class manuscript to Scholastic's *Kids Are Authors* program. Some offer a lovely mix of topics and approaches from students of various ages. *We Dream of a World ...* seems perfect for this chapter. It could be the final project in the class after students have examined the present Earth and its people. These young authors invite the reader to extend the dream by using the template at the end of the book.

The second book is a brief examination of time capsules. Siebert presents the artifacts discovered in China and Egypt as a type of time capsule. She then shares a number of time capsules that modern humans have prepared for future unveiling. Students might create a time capsule to represent the present and offer plans for the future.

### Other

- Gifted and Talented Students of Pershing Accelerated School. (2001). *We Dream of a World...* New York: Scholastic, Inc.
- Siebert, Patricia. (2002). *We Were Here: A Short History of Time Capsules*. Brookfield, CT: The Millbrook Press.

### *Layers*

Any given location on Earth has layers of history. The location has changed over time as a result of human and environmental factors, as well as the importance of the location. First graders study "Then and Now" in many school districts. This is usually not specific to a given location but is an introduction to the concept. As students move to third or fourth grade, they examine their community, county, and/or state. These units examine specific locations with an eye to Then and Now.

Baker's *Home* looks at one location through a bedroom window. The urban neighborhood surrounding home changes as neighbors take positive action over two decades. Burton's classic *The Little House* examines the community around the little house as it changes from rural to suburban to urban before the little house is moved back to a rural setting. *Pioneer Church,* based on a real church in Pennsylvania, tells the story of a building and how its importance changed over time.

*A Street Through Time* and *A Farm Through Time* are part of a series that examines specific locations over centuries. Extraordinary detailed color illustrations make these fascinating to students and adults. Both books are set in Europe. Macaulay's whimsical *Rome Antics* leads the reader on a tour of modern day Rome that includes ancient buildings that make layers of history visible. Yolen's *House, House* is a favorite. She and her son Jason Stemple collaborated to show photos, taken 100 years apart, of the same houses in their hometown of Hatfield, Massachusetts. The narrative compares life in the community at the time of the photos.

*A Gift from the Sea* and *On This Spot* explore the layers of time from right now to millions of years ago. The reader takes the journey with a rock found at the shore in *A Gift from the Sea* but stands still in a specific spot in New York City to move back in time in Goodman's book. Both books are intriguing but could use a timeline (one is found at the end of Goodman's books) to truly help students put the time in context.

## Layers

- Baker, Jeannie. (2004). *Home.* New York: Greenwillow Books.
- Banks, Kate. (2001). *A Gift from the Sea.* New York: Frances Foster Books.
- Burton, Virginia Lee. (1941/1969). *The Little House.* Boston: Houghton Mifflin Company.
- Goodman, Susan E. (2004). *On This Spot: An Expedition Back Through Time.* New York: Greenwillow Books.
- Macaulay, David. (1997). *Rome Antics.* Boston: Houghton Mifflin Company.
- Millard, Anne. (1998). *A Street Through Time.* London: Dorling Kindersley Ltd.
- Otto, Carolyn. (1999). *Pioneer Church.* New York: Henry Holt and Company.
- Wilkes, Angela. (2001). *A Farm Through Time.* New York: A Dorling Kindersley Book.
- Yolen, Jane. (1998). *House, House.* New York: Marshall Cavendish.

# Egypt

There are several newer texts about Egypt for younger readers. Bunting's work is really beautiful but less concrete, so it requires teacher support for younger students but is worthy nonetheless. Ms. Frizzle takes a vacation to Egypt and carries her fellow travelers back to ancient Egypt in typical faction fun. Each of Cole's Ms. Frizzle books tells a fictional story as it imparts factual information. Logan's is another student-friendly trip to Egypt in the 1920s through the eyes of a young boy whose family joins an archeological dig. Gibbons and Simon provide excellent informational books for young students.

## Egypt

- Bunting, Eve. (1997). *I Am the Mummy Heb-Nefret.* New York: Harcourt Brace.
- Cole, Joanna. (2002). *Ms. Frizzle's Adventures: Ancient Egypt.* New York: Scholastic.
- Gibbons, Gail. (2004). *Mummies, Pyramids, and Pharaohs: A Book about Ancient Egypt.* Boston: Little, Brown.
- Logan, Claudia (2004). *The 5,000-Year-Old Puzzle: Solving a Mystery of Ancient Egypt.* New York: Scholastic.
- Simon, Seymour. (2004). *Pyramids & Mummies.* New York: Scholastic.

# Teaching Ideas—Lesson Plans and Extension/Application Activities

The lesson plans and extensions in this chapter are taken from Kathy Boyle's presentations in the Primary Sources workshop at the Monroe County Historical Association (MCHA) in Stroudsburg, Pennsylvania. The first lesson uses artifacts from MCHA's collection. The second lesson uses photographs from the collection.

Kathy generally selects artifacts from the late nineteenth or early twentieth century for undergraduate students to examine. Among the artifacts are a fourth-grade math book published in the early 1900s, an ice skating blade that straps to a shoe, a noise-maker, a railroad spike, and a slate. Students work in groups of three or four, examining a total of six to eight artifacts.

When selecting artifacts, consider items that are at least 25 years old. For primary grade students—this is old! Select artifacts that represent goods or services classifications and that represent various areas in daily life such as tools, toys, school materials, clothing, and the like.

## *Lesson Plan 6.1—Artifacts*

### LEVELS: GRADE 2 (WHOLE GROUP ACTIVITY), GRADES 3 & 4

### Learning Goals

- Students will differentiate between making observations and inferences.
- Students will analyze and interpret data gathered from artifacts.
- Students will categorize artifacts in goods or services classifications.

### Assessment

- Informal Assessment: Observation of discussion and presentation of data.
- Formal Assessment: Artifacts Worksheet.
    - +3 Worksheet has detailed sketch and description using color, shape, texture, size, and materials
    - +2 Worksheet has sketch and description using at least three of preceding categories
    - +1 Worksheet is missing sketch or description; contains no details

### Materials

- selection of artifacts—place each in a brown paper bag
- Artifact Worksheets (one per small group)
- Artifact Worksheet transparency
- Artifact Sort Table transparency

### Key Questions and/or Vocabulary

- artifacts: physical examples of a culture such as tools, clothing, and food
- observation: gathering of data using the five senses
- inference: making educated guesses based on gathered data
- goods: products created and sold such as food items or clothing
- services: help provided at a cost by an expert or professional such as a doctor or plumber

### Procedure

#### *Motivation and Explanation*

- Begin by reviewing the terms goods and services. Encourage students to identify a variety of goods and services that impact their lives. Use concrete examples.
- Ask them if people have always had goods and services. Clarify that in earlier times people traded goods and services without formally exchanging money, called bartering; define the term barter.
- Ask students how they might determine what goods and services were available in past times. Guide students to think about reading old diaries, newspapers, and the like, as well as actually examining items from the past. Use and define the term artifacts.

### Demonstration and Modeling

- Show students an everyday object from the classroom. For example, hold up a color marker. Remind students that objects from today might be examined by historians or scientists 100 years in the future. Point out that when they examine artifacts they do so in two steps: First they observe; then they use their other senses. Ask which sense they think should be avoided. (Answer: taste) Why?
- Draw the marker on the Artifact Worksheet on the overhead transparency. Use a think-aloud strategy as you create the sketch.
- Continue using a think-aloud strategy to describe the marker with words. Point out to the students that the goal is to use observation skills to describe the marker and not to describe what the marker does.

### Guided Practice

- Have students help create the description. Use the senses and the prompts on the worksheet to focus the description. Use descriptive adjectives.
- Demonstrate making an inference. For example, say "When this top is removed, there is a pointed, moist portion. Rubbing it across the paper makes a mark. The marker fits in my hand and resembles a pencil. Do you think this marker might be a writing instrument?"
- Record students' observations and inferences on the Artifact Worksheet overhead transparency.

### Independent Practice

- Distribute artifacts placed in brown paper bags to reduce distraction. Give one bag to each small group of students.
- Give students several minutes to discuss artifacts. Monitor and ask open-ended questions where needed.
- Have students complete the Artifact Worksheet.

### Closure/Reflection

- Have each group share its findings with whole class.
- Use the Artifact Sort transparency to gather data from the students as they make their presentations to the class. Consider using the following questions to guide the final discussion:

  - "Is the item in use today? If not, why not? Has something replaced it?"
  - "Who might have used the item?"
  - "Did this person provide a good or service in the community?"
    Examine the data collected on the Artifact Sort transparency.
    Ask, "What are the ways to categorize these items?" Complete after group and whole-class presentations. Categories can be based on any variety of criteria that is reasonable, such as use, physical features, tool for agriculture, industry, home, etc.

## *Extension/Application Activity 6.1*

### LEVEL: GRADES 3 AND 4

The following activities can be used for enrichment activities or independent work. Students may work individually or in small groups.

- Create a catalog of the artifacts. Have each student (or small group) draw an item and write a descriptive caption. Compile the pages and bind the catalog.
- Write an ad for the item. Evaluate on appropriateness to context of time period. Display ads.
- Personify an artifact. Have students write a life story (3–5 sentences) for the artifact, including what it observed or experienced. Evaluate student's adherence to the context of the time period.
- Create a timeline of artifacts. It is easier for younger students to arrange items of the same category: lighting, tools, clothing, etc. Students can locate pictures in magazines of items used for the same purpose over time. Have students arrange pictures or artifacts in chronological order. Students can research items and add appropriate dates.

Students' favorite lesson in the Primary Sources Workshop is the one in which Kathy shares photographs from MCHA's archives. Kathy includes photos of local scenes that students may have visited or sites or businesses they recognize. Select photographs from your local community, or use the Library of Congress or National Geographic websites to find photographs.

## *Lesson Plan 6.2—Photographs: Getting the Whole Picture*

### LEVEL: GRADE 2 (WHOLE GROUP ACTIVITY), GRADES 3 AND 4

### Learning Goals

- Students will identify the elements of a selected photograph.
- Students will draw inferences based on observations.
- Students will identify economic activities in the community.
- Students will differentiate between human and physical aspects of place.
- Students will identify the point of view of the photographer.

### Assessment

- Informal Assessment: Observation of discussion about each photograph and completed Photographs: Getting the Whole Picture Note Page

### Materials

- *House, House* by Jane Yolen
- small magnifying glasses, if available
- photocopies of photographs in plastic sleeves (or laminate them)
- overhead transparencies of photographs (if possible, photocopies of photographs from two time periods such as the late 1800s and contemporary photographs of the same locations)
- Photographs: Getting the Whole Picture Note Page (This reproducible page has two sides.)
- Photographs: Getting the Whole Picture Note Page overhead transparency

### Key Questions and/or Vocabulary

- artifacts
- goods and services

### Procedure

#### *Motivation and Explanation*

- Gather students on the floor for a read-aloud experience with the *House, House* book. Be sure to read the author's preface, which explains the source of the photographs included in the book. Encourage students to compare and contrast the details in the photos.

#### *Demonstration and Modeling*

- Tell students that Jane Yolen used information from the Howe Brothers' photographs to help her think about what she wanted to learn about life in Hatfield, Massachusetts, 100 years ago.
- Tell students they will look at some photos of (name a community) and see what they can learn from them.

### Guided Practice

- Display an overhead transparency of one of the photographs.
- Encourage students to work with a partner to generate a list of people, objects, and activities they can see.
- Get feedback from the class and record their observations on the Photographs: Getting the Whole Picture transparency.

  - Ask, "Does the photograph tell anything else?"
  - Consider physical environment: weather, season, day of week, etc.
  - Consider economic activity: evidence of goods and services.

- Ask students to think about their community today. How is it the same as the photograph? How is it different?
- Ask students to speculate as to changes. For example, ask, "How have humans modified the environment? How have tastes and values changed? Are the goods and/or services obsolete? Are there outside influences that caused change?"
- Examine the point of view of the photographer.

  What was the purpose?
  Why was it shot the way it was?
  Would the impression have been the same if the photograph was shot differently?

### Independent Practice

Distribute photocopies of other photographs to pairs or triads of students.
Distribute the Photographs: Getting the Whole Picture Note Page.

### Closure/Reflection

Have each group share their notes about their photograph.
Encourage the other students to make observations and ask questions.

## Extension/Application Activity 6.2—Compare and Contrast Change Over Time
### LEVEL: GRADES 2 (WHOLE GROUP ACTIVITY), GRADES 3 AND 4

A. This activity might be a new lesson or a project at a center.

- Select 2–3 photographs of the same subject matter (transportation, school, family, shelter, tools). For example, the three photos shown here identify modes of transportation around Glencoe, Illinois, in the early 1900s. It is a community on the north shore of Lake Michigan about 25 miles north of Chicago, In the early 1900s, a farmer would drive his horse and wagon loaded with horseradish roots from Glencoe into Chicago to sell to the Plockman Company (they made mustard and horseradish). It took a full day to complete the roundtrip. Two of the photos were taken at the Glencoe train station; the other one is outside a home (See Figure 6.1). Use photocopies of photographs from your community or download photographs from the

**Figure 6.1**  Modes of transportation in Glencoe, Illinois.

(*continued*) **Figure 6.1**    Modes of transportation in Glencoe, Illinois.

Library of Congress or National Geographic Web sites. Newspaper archives and historical associations often have wonderful photos that can be duplicated. Send home a note to parents asking for copies of old photographs of the local community.
- Place the photocopies in a 6 × 9-inch envelope labeled with the subject matter to be observed.
- Have several packets of photographs available so that several students can work independently or in small groups.
- Have students determine how the photographs are similar and different. Provide copies of a blank Venn diagram to be used with two of the photos.
- On the back of the Venn diagram have students answer these questions:

  - Why do you think the changes occurred?
  - Are the changes good? Why? Why not?

   B. A second activity might include more than two or three photos in the same packet to be examined on the following prompts:

- Sequence the photographs from earliest to most recent.
- Ask students in which time period they would like to live and why. Choose one of the following writing assignments:

- In three to five sentences, explain why you made the choice.
- Create a newspaper ad promoting your choice.

## *Extension Application Activity 6.3—Poetry*

### LEVEL: GRADES 3 AND 4

Help your students transform the information they collected in Lesson Plan 6.2 from factual data to an aesthetic response using this modified diamante poetry format. Center each line of the poem in the final draft. It will then have a diamond shape.

Line 1: subject—one noun
Line 2: two adjectives describing the subject
Line 3: three participles (-ing) telling about the subject
Line 4: four nouns telling about the subject
Line 5: one noun—another word for Line 1

The following poem is an example using another photo from the Glencoe photos. This unidentified young man is dressed to receive customers, but there is no description for the photograph. Could this be his first day on the job and the family documented it with a photograph? Has he just taken over the business?

shopkeeper

formal, young

standing, showing, selling

salesman, proprietor, leader, worker

owner

This lesson includes two books that provide interesting information about cave paintings. The first book is *Talking Walls,* which includes two simple selections about cave paintings: one is the Lascaux Caves discovered in 1940; the other is an Aboriginal cave painting in Australia. The second book, *Painters of the Caves,* examines the paintings found in 1994 by three French cave explorers. The Internet also provides several sites with beautiful photos of cave paintings that can be downloaded; search using the term *Lascaux Caves.*

**Figure 6.2**   Shopkeeper.

## Lesson Plan 6.3—Visual Clues in Cave Paintings

LEVEL: GRADES 1, 2, AND 3

### Learning Goals

- Students will explain why researchers are interested in cave art.
- Students will offer probable cave painting messages.
- Students will create messages about their lives for future researchers to discover.

### Assessment

- Informal Assessment: Observation of discussion

### Materials

- *Talking Walls* by Margy Burns Knight
- *Painters of the Caves* by Patricia Lauber
- brown paper (9 × 12-inch) or use butcher paper cut into individual pieces for students
- white tempera paint
- table salt
- oil pastels "craypas"—use only red, orange, yellow, brown, and black
- #10 paint brushes
- paper towels
- cave art printout reproductions from Internet

### Key Questions and/or Vocabulary

- artifacts
- cave paintings
- calcify/calcification
- archeologists
- anthropologists

### Procedure

#### Motivation and Explanation

- Gather students to listen to a read-aloud. Use either *Painters of the Caves* or *Talking Walls* by Margy Burns Knight. If reading *Painters of the Caves*, read only parts of the book for this lesson.
- Show the illustrations while reading the book. Make the read-aloud interactive by asking questions to guide thinking and accepting comments and questions.
- Return to the pages that explain the Lascaux Cave paintings and the Aborigine wall paintings.
- Ask students to predict how old the paintings are. (These paintings are thousands of years old and were created by prehistoric painters.)
- Ask students to describe what they see in the picture and what is happening. Prompt as needed.
- Display photos from *Painters of the Caves* or Internet printouts (or other sources you may have located). Ask students what they see and what actions are taking place in the paintings.

- Inform students that prehistoric painters used their paintings as a way to display an event, thought, or feeling.
- Ask students why the prehistoric painters used the walls instead of paper. Tell students that these artists did not have paper or all the colors available today; they had only red, brown, yellow, orange, and black. They had to make their own paints from materials they found in nature.
- Let students know that today they will create cave paintings in the style of prehistoric painters that show an animal or an event.

### Demonstration and Modeling

- Show students how to tear the edges of the brown paper so that it looks like a cave wall.
- Model for students how to crumble the paper into a ball a few times, then to gently smooth it out. Tell students this is to give it a more textured look, like a cave wall.
- Use a pencil to sketch the shape of an animal on your paper. Explain why you have selected the animal and how you are showing an event.

### Guided Practice

- Have students write their names on the back of their paper, then crumble it.
- Smooth the wrinkles of the paper, and have students draw the outline of an animal.
- Have each student chose one colored pastel. Tell students that brown will be used as the first layer of color on your paper. Have students fill in their shape with their chosen color.
- Tell students they will need to blend the brown color with the red pastel. If they press a little harder the colors blend better. (Demonstrate this process.) Have students follow along with their second color of choice.
- Have students watch as you add a third and final color to your animal drawing.
- Demonstrate the dabbling of white paint around the edge of their drawings, using a paper towel. Calcify the paint by sprinkling table salt on the wet paint.

### Independent Practice

- Circulate to assist students as they complete their color drawing with the third oil pastel color.
- Allow students to dabble white paint (not excessively) around the edge of the drawing and sprinkle the salt. Excess salt can be shaken off over a garbage can.

### Closure/Reflection

- Discuss what future historians, archeologists, or scientists might learn about them by looking at their "cave paintings."
- Display the students' paintings with explanations attached.

# References

Wiggins, Grant P., and McTighe, Jay. (1998). *Understanding by Design.* Upper Saddle River, NJ: Prentice Hall.

# Artifact Worksheet

**OBSERVATION**

1. Sketch the artifact. You might want to show it from two view points.




2. Examine the artifact using your sense of sight, touch, hearing, and smell. **Do not taste it!** Use describing words to create a word picture.

Think about:
- color

- shape

- size

- texture

- shape

- materials

**INFERENCE**

What is this object? How was it used? Is it still used today?

## Artifact Sort Table

| Artifact? | Goods or Service? | Use? |
|---|---|---|
|  |  |  |
|  |  |  |
|  |  |  |
|  |  |  |
|  |  |  |
|  |  |  |
|  |  |  |
|  |  |  |

# Photographs: Getting the Whole Picture Note Page

1. Work with a partner to generate a list of people, objects, and activities you can see.
- Consider physical environment: weather, season, day of week, etc.
- Consider economic activity: evidence of goods and services.




2. Think about our community today.
- How is it the same as the photograph?
- How is it different?

Photographs: Getting the Whole Picture Note Page

3. Think about the changes:
- How have humans modified their environment?
- How have tastes and values changed?
- Are the goods and services obsolete?
- Do you observe outside influences, etc?

4. Examine the point of view of the photographer.
- What was the purpose?
- Why was it shot the way it
- Would the impression have been the same is shot differently? was?

# Annotated Bibliography

This bibliography contains more than 200 books. As mentioned in the Introduction, I examined each book included here. They have either been reprinted or are still in print despite their older date of publication. Only two published before 1999 are no longer in print and are indicated by an asterisk (*). Each entry contains a summary paragraph followed by the chapter in which it appears in a text set.

## Children's Literature

Aardema, Verna. (1992). *Bringing the Rain to Kapiti Plain.* New York: Puffin Books. This tale, discovered in Kenya, Africa, more than 70 years ago, is reminiscent of "The House That Jack Built." Aardema has brought the story closer to the English nursery rhyme by putting in a cumulative refrain and giving it the nursery rhyme's rhythm, making it particularly appropriate for reading aloud. Large color illustrations enhance the text. Chapter 2—Same and Different Around the World: Africa

Adler, David A. (2003). *A Picture Book of Lewis and Clark.* New York: Holiday House. Adler's account of the Lewis and Clark expedition provides the young reader with an introduction to the lives of the explorers and the unique contribution they made to the new nation. Colorful illustrations accompany the text, which is rich with journal quotations. A map of the explored territory provided at the beginning of the book gives the reader a sense of this vast undertaking. Adler provides brief notes at the end of the book as well as important dates related to the expedition. Chapter 4—Exploration

Aliki. (1998). *Marianthe's Story: Painted Words; Marianthe's Story: Spoken Memories.* New York: Greenwillow Books. This unique book tells two stories about the same young girl. Marianthe tells the story of her experiences in a new country and school through her daily drawings until she is finally able to make sense of the new world around her. In the second story she tells her classmates the story of her family's life in their old country before they moved to the United States. Aliki's gentle words and full-color pencil and crayon drawings model how important understanding and acceptance are as we embark on new and unknown experiences. Chapter 4—Immigration

Amis, Nancy. (2003). *The Orphans of Normandy: A True Story of World War II Told Through Drawings by Children.* New York: Atheneum Books for Young Readers. Translated quotes by 100 orphan girls forced to flee from their orphanage in Caen to Beaufort-en-Vallee. Drawings tell the story of their 150-mile journey on foot to safety. Children's quotes face the page of their illustrations throughout the book. In an Afterward, Nancy Amis explains that these came from her aunt, Agnes Amis, whose friend, Yvonne Lescure, the directress of a school in Caen, France, sent after the war. Chapter 4—World War II: Europe

Ammon, Richard. (2000). *An Amish Christmas.* New York: Aladdin Paperbacks. A young Amish boy tells the story of his family's Christmas celebration in first-person narrative. The story includes the events at school on Christmas Eve and the family celebration on Christmas Day. As he shares the joys of this simple Christmas observation, the reader learns about the other daily chores and interactions in the Amish farm life. Beautiful pastel drawings provide visual images supporting the text. Chapter 4—Cultural Mosaics: Other

Arnosky, Jim. (1998). *Watching Desert Wildlife.* Washington, D.C.: National Geographic Society. Arnosky shares his eye-opening discoveries during his first visit to the desert of the American Southwest through personal narrative. Observing both as naturalist and artist, he is able to combine his knowledge and talent to organize this informational book by category such as snakes or desert squirrels and unique animals such as the Gila monster and roadrunner. Each informational page is faced by a full-page detailed color painting of the animal/s in its/their habitat, expanding the text. Chapter 3—Ecosystems: Desert

Arnosky, Jim. (2000). *Wild and Swampy.* New York: HarperCollins Publishers. Full-page acrylic paintings and journal-style pen and ink drawings accompany Arnosky's descriptive narrative about the swamps in the American South. The text describes the flora and fauna of the swamps plus tips about how to spot wildlife. Chapter 3—Ecosystems: Swamp

Bailey, Jacqui. (2004). *Sun up, Sun down: The Story of Day and Night.* Minneapolis, MN: Picture Window Books. Informational book that follows the sun from dawn to dusk to explain how light rays travel, how shadows are formed, how the moon lights up the night sky, and more. Cartoon-like drawings and diagrams illustrate the text. An index is included. Chapter 3—Earth's Systems: Nonfiction

Baker, Jeannie. (2004). *Home.* New York: Greenwillow Books. The life of a baby, Tracy, and her neighborhood are observed through the child's window. Baker's striking natural collages document the way an urban community reclaims the neighborhood. The drab surroundings become a beautiful environment in which families live and thrive. Chapter 5—Human/Environmental Interaction; Chapter 6—Layers

Banks, Kate. (2001). *A Gift from the Sea.* New York: Frances Foster Books. A boy finds a rock and, unaware of its eons-old history, takes it home and places it on a shelf beside his sea glass and starfish. Richly colored full-page paintings complement the text as it tells of the journey of the rock—from the time when dinosaurs lived, through the ice age and early civilization, from the mouth of a volcano to the bottom of the ocean and onto the beach. Reminiscent of George Ella Lyon's *Who Came Down That Road?*, this book demonstrates "layers" of history in a given location or object. Chapter 6—Layers

Banks, Sara H. (1997). *A Net to Catch Time.* New York: Alfred A. Knopf. Cuffy, a young Gullah boy, wants to earn enough money to buy a boat. Living on one of Georgia's barrier islands, Cuffy spends his day marked by the unique Gullah times of the day from *first fowl crow* of five-thirty in the morning to *candle-light time* at seven in the evening—twilight. The soft pastel drawings enhance the story of Cuffy's work ethic and close-knit family. Chapter 3—Earth's Systems: Fiction

Bates, Katharine Lee. (1993). *America the Beautiful.* New York: Antheneum Books for Young Readers. Neil Waldman was inspired to illustrate the first verse of this patriotic song by a huge rectangular trip beginning in New York, west through the northern Rockies to the Pacific Northwest, then down the entire Pacific Coast and back through the Southwest and South. Fourteen full-page acrylic paintings show human-made wonders such as Mount Rushmore, ancient dwellings of the Mesa Verde, and natural wonders like the Grand Canyon. Thumbnail images with descriptions of the exact locations are included at the end of the book. Chapter 2—Tour the USA: Aesthetic

Bates, Katharine Lee. (2003). *America the Beautiful.* New York: G. P. Putnam's Sons. Wendell Minor has illustrated all four verses of this patriotic song with 21 watercolor and gouache landscape paintings that represent the images that come to mind when he sings the words. Small oval presentations of the paintings are presented with the illustrator's explanation for each inclusion in the book. A U.S. map identifies the location that inspired each painting. Chapter 2—Tour the USA: Aesthetic

Bates, Katharine Lee. (2004). *America the Beautiful.* New York: Little, Brown and Company. Chris Gall, the great-great-grandnephew of Katherine Lee Bates, has illustrated the first verse of this patriotic song with 16 moments in history unique to the American spirit and experience. The illustrations were created by hand engraving clay-coated board, followed by digitizing with Adobe Illustrator for adjustments and color. Thumbnail images with informational paragraphs are provided at the end of the book. Chapter 2—Tour the USA: Aesthetic

Bearden, Romare. (2003). *Li'l Dan the Drummer Boy: A Civil War Story.* New York: Simon & Schuster Books for Young Readers. Although published after the author's death, this Civil War story was written and illustrated by Romare Bearden in the 1970s. Li'l Dan doesn't understand what freedom means when a company of black Union soldiers come to the plantation where he lives. Since he has no place to go, Li'l Dan decides to follow the soldiers who make him their mascot. He carries the drum he had made and learned to play with the help of Old Ned, another slave. Li'l Dan's clever mind and drum help him save his new friends from a Confederate attack. Brightly colored mixed media illustrations enhance the text. Chapter 4—Civil War

Bierman, Carol. (1998). *Journey to Ellis Island: How My Father Came to America*. Toronto: Madison Press Books. In this "faction" book, Carol Bierman tells the story of her father's immigration to America in 1922 through a third-person narrative. Enhancing and expanding the personal story are photographs and reproductions of postcards with informational captions about the process at Ellis Island through which many immigrants passed between 1880 and 1914. Chapter 4—Immigration

Blake, Robert. (2002). *Togo*. New York: Philomel Books. Man's struggle with Nature is the focus of this riveting story of Togo, an Alaskan husky considered too small to be a good sled dog. But Togo proved to have incredible stamina and a keen sense of direction that was needed when Nome, Alaska, was on the brink of a diphtheria epidemic in January 1925. Blake's powerful oil paintings combine with his text to keep the reader on the edge of his/her seat waiting to hear the outcome of this true story. Chapter 3—Ecosystems: Arctic; Chapter 5—Climate/Weather

Blumberg, Rhoda (2004). *York's Adventures with Lewis and Clark: An African-American's Part in the Great Expedition*. New York: HarperCollins Publishers. This informative biography of York, William Clark's slave, offers a rich and unusual look at the Lewis and Clark expedition with special note of York's contribution. Using Clark's journal, Blumberg reveals York's importance. The 76 illustrations selected by Blumberg for this book come from historical and art institutions across the country. While intended for a school-age audience, the book would be effective for primary-age students if used as a read-aloud. Chapter 4—Exploration

Borden, Louise. (1997). *The Little Ships: The Heroic Rescue at Dunkirk in World War II*. New York: Margaret K. McElderry Books. This small book with beautiful watercolor illustrations tells the story of the brave Englishmen who crossed the English Channel in a flotilla of small river and coastal boats. Borden tells the story through the first person account of a young girl who dresses in her brother's clothes and sails with her father on their family boat, *The Lucy*. While most of the Allied soldiers trapped on the French coast by German tanks and troops were transported by the bigger ships, the little ships ferried the hungry and exhausted soldiers during a nine-day period in 1940 from the Dunkirk beaches across the dangers shallow water to the big ships. Chapter 4—World War II: Europe

Brown, Dan. (1997). *Alice Ramsey's Grand Adventure*. Boston: Houghton Mifflin, Co. In 1906, Alice Ramsey set out with her friend and two sisters-in-law to drive from New York City to San Francisco to become the first woman to drive across America. The "grand adventure," with Alice as the only one of the travelers who knew about automobiles, took 59 days. Brown's watercolor illustrations provide delightful visual documentation of the variety of challenges and adventures the trip entailed. Chapter 4—Transportation: Land

Brown, Don. (1998). *One Giant Leap: The Story of Neil Armstrong*. Boston: Houghton Mifflin Company. Pen-and-ink and watercolor illustrations enrich the story of Neil Armstrong whose fascination with flying began in his early years. Neil took his first airplane ride when he was six years old. As he grew he made airplane models, read flying magazines, and had magical dreams of hovering. Despite his busy life engaged in school, Boy Scouts, and school band, Neil worked to earn enough money to take flying lessons. He earned his student pilot's license at age 16, going on to become a navy fighter pilot in the Korean War, a test pilot, and an astronaut—the first man to walk on the moon! Chapter 4—Exploration; Transportation: Air

Brown, Don. (2000). *Uncommon Traveler: Mary Kingsley in Africa.* New York: Houghton Mifflin Company. Mary Kingsley, a self-educated young English woman, decided to travel through unexplored West Africa after the deaths of her parents in 1892. A remarkable journey for anyone in 1893 and 1894, Mary's journey, in which she gathered information and specimens that she later donated to the British Museum of Natural History, was extraordinary for a woman. While "traveling light" and wearing high-necked, long-sleeved shirts, long heavy skirts, and proper Victorian boots, she successfully explored the mysterious region and returned to England to write and lecture about her experiences. Watercolor paintings illustrate Mary's adventures. Chapter 4—Exploration

Bruchac, Joseph. (2000). *Squanto's Journey: The Story of the First Thanksgiving.* San Diego: Silver Whistle—Harcourt, Inc. Squanto shares his life story in this beautifully illustrated book. Unlike the usual approach to the story of the first Thanksgiving, Bruchac provides the reader with Squanto's life before the Pilgrim story begins and tells the story of the Pilgrim community's first year's struggle to survive from Squanto's point of view. A rich author's note and simple glossary are included at the end of the book. Chapter 4—Immigration; Cultural Mosaics: Native American

Bruchac, Joseph. (2004). *Many Nations: An Alphabet of Native America.* New York: Scholastic, Inc. The simple text in this beautiful alphabet book introduces the reader to the many native tribes from the Anishinabe to the Micmac to the Zuni who represent the hundreds of surviving nations of Native America. Full-page color illustrations honor the beauty and diversity of Native American cultures. This book is a wonderful place to introduce students to the rich past and present cultures of the indigenous people of North America. Chapter 4—Cultural Mosaics: Native American

Bruchac, Joseph and London, Jonathan. (1992). *Thirteen Moons on Turtle's Back: A Native American Year of Moons.* New York: Scholastic, Inc. Sozap's grandfather shares the secret of keeping track of the year by counting the 13 moons on the turtle's back. The Abenaki grandfather explains how the knowledge is passed down through the generations. He admits that other Native people have moons. Each of the 13 moons (based on the moon's 28-day cycle) is described by different nations representing different regions of the continent. Gentle color paintings complement the text. Chapter 3—Earth's Systems: Fiction; Chapter 4—Cultural Mosaics: Native American

Bulion, Leslie. (2002). *Fatuma's New Cloth.* North Kingstown, RI: Moon Mountain Publishing. Little Fatuma helps her mother with the day's marketing and learns a lesson about not judging something by its outward appearance. Inspired by her own travels in East Africa, Bulion takes the reader to an authentic African market in words while the beautiful, whimsical watercolor paintings offer kanka cloth borders around the illustrations. Chapter 2—Same and Different Around the World: Africa

Bunting, Eve. (1996). *Train to Somewhere.* New York: Scholastic, Inc. Marianne is one of 14 children traveling by train from New York City to Somewhere, Iowa. Along the way the train stops so that the children can get off to be examined, and perhaps chosen to join a family. Marianne, who is older than the other children, hopes her mother will be waiting for her at one of the stops. Full-page color paintings complement the tense, yet hopeful, mood of this heartwarming story based on the orphan trains that ran from the mid-1850s until the late 1920s. Chapter 4—Westward Expansion

Bunting, Eve. (1997). *I Am the Mummy Heb-Nefret.* New York: Harcourt Brace & Company. In this strange yet compelling lyrical text, Heb-Nefret tells the story of her life long ago in Egypt. Richly colored watercolors enhance the story. Chapter 6—Egypt

Bunting, Eve. (1998). *So Far from the Sea.* New York: Clarion Books. Seven-year-old Laura Iwasaki and her family visit her grandfather's grave at the Manzanar War Relocation camp before a move to Massachusetts. As the family says farewell to Grandfather, Laura's father describes the camp during the years he and his parents lived there. His memories help Laura select the perfect memento to leave behind on the grave. Beautiful full-page watercolors tell the current story while dramatic sepia paintings portray Laura's father's memories. Chapter 4—World War II

Bunting, Eve. (2001). *Jin Woo.* New York: Clarion Books. Young David has doubts about how the arrival of an adopted baby from Korea can be a good event. Beautiful full-page watercolors join Bunting's text in bringing deep emotion to this moving story. As David comes to understand how his parents can have enough love for more than one child, the family also begins to acknowledge how they can make sure Jin Woo doesn't lose his Korean heritage in his new American family. Chapter 4—Immigration

Bunting, Eve. (2006). *One Green Apple.* New York: Clarion Books. Farah is new to the United States and finds the class trip to the apple orchard offers her a chance to interact with her classmates. Despite the language and cultural barriers, Farah and Anne find ways to communicate. Encouraged by the experience, Farah is hopeful. Ted Lewin's rich full-page watercolors join Bunting's sensitive text to put the reader into the shoes of this young Muslim immigrant. Chapter 4—Immigration

Bunting, Eve. (2006). *Pop's Bridge.* Orlando: Harcourt, Inc. Robert's father is one of the ironworkers building the Golden Gate Bridge. Although his friend, Charlie, is also proud of his father, a painter on the bridge, Robert cannot imagine that Charlie's dad is as important to the project as his own. After a tragic event, Robert recognizes the importance of teamwork on such an enormous project. Full-color multimedia illustrations complement Bunting's text. The author's note at the end provides interesting historical information. Chapter 5—Construction/Architecture

Burleigh, Robert. (1991). *Flight: The Journey of Charles Lindbergh.* New York: Trumpet Club Special Edition. This book, based on Lindbergh's own account of his historic flight from New York to Paris in 1927, tells of the long transatlantic flight through full-color illustrations and narrative. The reader has a unique perspective because eye levels for the illustrations are in nontraditional places, such as viewing the airplane before the flight from between Lindbergh's legs. The introduction by author Jean Fritz helps the reader understand Lindbergh's status as national hero. Chapter 4—Transportation: Air

Burton, Virginia Lee. (1942/1969). *The Little House.* Boston: Houghton Mifflin Company. This delightful Caldecott Medal winner tells the story of the changes in the life of the little house and her whole community. The color illustrations and text describe the change in the community from rural to urban through the eyes of the little house. Chapter 4—Lesson Plan 4.3; Chapter 6—Layers

Busby, Peter. (2002). *First to Fly: How Wilber & Orville Wright Invented the Airplane.* Toronto: A Scholastic/Madison Press Book. Full-page paintings, photographs, and diagrams accompany a text rich with information about the Wright brothers' amazing accomplishment. The book provides background information about the brothers' lives and how they came to accomplish what men had dreamed of for centuries: flight! The captions under the photos as well as informational sidebars provide background and/or extensions to the book's narrative. Chapter 4—Transportation: Air

Cave, Kathryn. (1998). *W Is for World: A Round-the-World ABC.* London, Great Britain: Frances Lincoln Children's Books. Photos accompany text that offers both human and physical characteristics of more than 20 countries around the world from Greenland to Vietnam. Written with the support of Oxfam, this book is intended to encourage everyone to make a difference in the lives of children around the world through support for food, shelter, health care, and education. Chapter 2—Same and Different Around the World: General

Cheney, Lynne. (2004). *When Washington Crossed the Delaware: A Wintertime Story for Young Patriots.* New York: Simon & Schuster Books for Young Readers. Cheney relates the events that led to a pivotal moment in the life of our young country with rich details that are reflected in the beautiful oil paintings. Clearly written descriptive paragraphs call for a dramatic read-aloud presentation. The quotations presented through the text are referenced at the end of the book. The end papers depict a map of Washington's plan of the operation. Chapter 4—Revolutionary War

Cherry, Lynne. (1992). *A River Ran Wild.* San Diego: A Gulliver Green Book. This book tells the environmental history of the Nashua River from its discovery by Indians through the polluting years of the Industrial Revolution to the ambitious cleanup that revitalized it. Full-page watercolor drawings face the text pages, which are bordered by illustrations of elements associated with the narrative. The author provides detailed information about the Nashua River Valley in the author's notes and on the endpapers and flyleafs. Chapter 2—Tasting Places in the USA; Chapter 3—Ecosystems: Rivers; Chapter 5—Human/Environmental Interaction

Cherry, Lynne. (1994). *The Armadillo from Amarillo*. San Diego: A Gulliver Green Book. A wandering armadillo, Sasparillo, sees some of the cities, historic sites, geographic features, and wildlife of Texas as he attempts to discover where in the world he is. Finally, aided by an eagle that soars far above the earth with Sasparillo on his back, the armadillo discovers he's in a city within a state that's one of 50 in a country that is on the North American continent on planet Earth. The story, told in verse, is accompanied by detailed, full-page watercolor drawings with postcards inset into the page, which add more information. The author's note and acknowledgment at the end of the book further expand its content. Chapter 2—Tasting Places in the USA

Cherry, Lynne. (2000). *The Great Kapok Tree: A Tale of the Amazon Rain Forest*. San Diego: Voyager Books Harcourt, Inc. A man with an ax comes into the rain forest with the intent of cutting down the great kapok tree. The work is so hot and tiring that he stops to rest, falling asleep. While he sleeps the inhabitants of the rain forest whisper in the man's ear. Each tells what a loss of the rain forest will mean to the world. Beautifully detailed, full-page color drawings accompany the text. The natural flora and fauna are in the drawings as well as on the endpapers and flyleafs. The endpapers and flyleafs also include a world map locating the rain forest as they previously existed and as they exist today. Chapter 3—Ecosystems: Rain Forest; Chapter 5—Human/Environmental Interaction

Cherry, Lynne, and Plotkin, Mark J. (1998). *The Shaman's Apprentice: A Tale of the Amazon Rain Forest*. San Diego: A Gulliver Green Book. Young Kamanya dreams of becoming the next shaman by learning from the Nahtahlah, the tribal shaman, but a sickness comes to the village that Nahtahlah cannot cure and Nahtahlah loses his place of honor. Fortunately, a foreigner arrives who helps the villagers understand the value of Nahtahlah's wisdom and Kamanya can realize his dream. Full-page watercolor illustrations support the text. Chapter 3—Ecosystems: Rain Forest; Chapter 5—Human/Environmental Interaction

Chin-Lee, Cynthia. (1997). *A Is for Asia*. New York: Orchard Books. This delightful alphabet book offers 26 informational paragraphs describing the variety of physical and human characteristics that make Asia a unique continent. Noting that the languages of Asia are as varied as the cultures and countries, Chin-Lee provides the words chosen to represent each letter written in the appropriate Asian language. Detailed pen, oil, and collage illustrations accompany the text. Chapter 2—Same and Different Around the World: Asia

Cole, Joanna. (2002). *Ms. Frizzle's Adventures: Ancient Egypt*. New York: Scholastic, Inc. Ms. Frizzle is off to Egypt for a summer trip. Much to her surprise and those of her fellow airline passengers, they depart the plane via parachutes and tour Ancient Egypt where they engage in hands-on learning. Bruce Degen's whimsical color illustrations and Joanna Cole's delightful mix of fiction and fact take the reader on an adventure to remember. Chapter 6—Egypt

Crane, Carol. (2003). *P Is for Pilgrim: a Thanksgiving Alphabet*. Chelsea, MI: Sleeping Bear Press. The history and lore of Thanksgiving is explored through the alphabet. This "faction" book can be read twice using the two text formats for each page. Rhyming verses provide the alphabet match with words from A for "Atlantic Ocean" to Z for "zippy bands" in the Thanksgiving Day parade. Informational sidebars expand the verse content. Full-page color paintings accompany the text. Chapter 4—Immigration

Crosbie, Michael J., Rosenthal, Steve and Rosenthal, Kit. (2000). *Arches to Zigzags: An Architecture ABC*. New York: Harry N. Abrams, Inc. Using intriguing photographs and clever rhymes, children are introduced to basic terms in architecture within a context. Each rhyme ends with a question to stimulate the reader's thinking. Thumbnail photos with informational paragraphs provide more information about the architectural term and where the photograph was taken. Chapter 5—Construction/Architecture

Dawes, Kwame. (2005). *I Saw Your Face*. New York: Dial Books. Dawes' lyrical text connects a beautiful collection of drawings of children's faces by award-winning artist Tom Feelings. The drawings, sketched over Feelings' career, reveal the history of the African Diaspora through faces of young people from around the world. Chapter 4—Cultural Mosaics: Distribution

DiPucchio, Kelly (2004). *Liberty's Journey*. New York: Hyperion Books for Children. Lady Liberty decides to find out what the immigrants she has welcomed for more than one hundred years have seen as they moved on across the nation. So, one morning she begins a journey of discovery. Caldecott winner Richard Egielski's illustrations expand the fantasy verse. A historical note about the creation and characteristics of this national monument is included at the end of the book. Chapter 2—Tasting Places in the USA

Dixon, Ann. (2002). *Winter Is*. Portland, OR: Alaska Northwest Books. Clever, simple rhymes describe the exciting characteristics of winter, especially for a child. Charming full-page watercolor paintings are a perfect match for the text. This book, set in Alaska, is a good introductory book for examining the winter season. Chapter 3—Earth's Systems: Fiction

Eduar, Gilles. (2002) *Gigi and Zachary's Around-the-World-Adventure: A Seek-and-Find Game*. San Francisco: Chronicle Books LLC. Originally published in France, this imaginary tale of Gigi the Giraffe and Zachary the Zebra tells of their visits to many places around the world. At each stop along the way, the reader is encouraged to find all the items in the colorful, cartoon-like illustrations. The 500 words included at the 20 locations are identified at the end of the book. A simple world map on the endpapers and flyleafs identifies the route of the journey beginning in an African savanna and ending on their dream island off the coast of North Africa. Chapter 2—Same and Different Around the World: General

Fifth-grade Students of Coast Episcopal School. (2004). *Color for Thought*. New York: Scholastic. In this *Kids Are Authors* book, 13 students from Long Beach, Mississippi created an interesting book that uncovers the sources for color in our lives from the clothes we wear to the food we eat. Color drawings and diagrams enhance the informative text. Readers are invited to engage in some hands-on experiences with color. An index and bibliography are also provided. Chapter 5—Human/Environmental Interaction

Fleischman, Paul. (2000). *Weslandia.* New York: Scholastic, Inc. Wesley just doesn't fit in. His parents recognize it and his classmates torment him. Even Wesley acknowledges that he's an outcast from the civilization around him. Wesley, however, begins a summer project during which he grows his own staple food crop and founds his own civilization, meeting all his needs. Full-page color illustrations and clever text display Wesley's remarkable accomplishment that turns around his life and his relationship with his peers. Chapter 5—Human/Environmental Interactions

Fourment, Tiffany. (2004). *My Water Comes from the Mountains.* Lanham, MD: Roberts Rinehart Publishers. This book introduces students to watersheds, the Continental Divide and how snowmelt in the mountains leads to life in the land below. The text also includes a description of the water cycle and a discussion about how we use water and treat it. Beautiful detailed ink and colored pencil drawings illustrate the text. Drawings and small colored illustrations created by third-grade students from a school in Boulder, Colorado, add to the content throughout the book. Chapter 3—Earth's Systems: Nonfiction

Fowler, Susi Gregg. (1998). *Circle of Thanks.* New York: Scholastic, Inc. The cycle of the seasons of the year shape this fictional/fantasy tale of a boy and his mother in the Arctic tundra. Subtle color paintings bring the flora and fauna to life as the text tells of the interdependence of the native Arctic animals. Chapter 3—Ecosystems: Arctic

Fradin, Dennis Brindell. (2005). *Let It Begin Here!: Lexington & Concord: First Battles of the American Revolution.* New York: Walker & Company. First the stage is set with a few introductory paragraphs. Then the 24 hours that changed a rebellious colony is described with brief, but dramatic text identified through date and time beginning with April 18, 1775, 9:30 P.M.—Paul Revere learns he must warn the colonist that the British are coming and ending with April 19, 1775, 7:00 P.M. as the British limp into Boston having been defeated in the first battle of the Revolutionary War. Powerful full-page watercolors complement the text. Additional information about the people on both sides of the battle as well as resources and further reading is provided for the reader. Chapter 4—Revolutionary War

Fuchs, Bernie. (2004). *Ride Like the Wind: A Tale of the Pony Express.* New York: The Blue Sky Press. Based on the wealth of pony express stories, Fuchs paints a story in dramatic words and powerful oil paintings of an exciting, important, and dangerous job unique to the development of the United States. Although it lasted only 19 months, the pony express employed young riders like Johnny Free, who carried the mail from St. Joseph, Missouri to Sacramento, California—nearly 2,000 miles. Johnny's confrontation with the Paiute people was a real threat to riders. Chapter 4—Transportation: Land

George, Jean Craighead. (1999). *Snow Bear.* New York: Hyperion Books for Children. Young Bessie Nivyek decides to climb aboard the huge block of ice pushed up from the Arctic Ocean near the shore. She doesn't realize her brother, Vincent, is keeping watch over her because he's seen bear tracks. Likewise, Snow Bear doesn't realize he's being followed by his mother, Nanuq, because she knows how dangerous humans can be to bears. The simple text and beautiful full-page color paintings tell a delightful tale of instant friendship. Chapter 3—Ecosystems: Arctic

George, Lindsay Barrett. (2006). *In the Garden: Who's Been Here?* New York: Greenwillow Books. As Jeremy and Christina pick vegetables for their mother, they see evidence of animals and insects that have been in the garden before them. Similar to her other "Who's Been Here" books, this lovely book contains beautifully detailed full-page paintings that introduce eight creatures native to many North American gardens. The simple text makes it accessible to young readers. Thumbnail paintings and descriptive paragraphs of each featured animal are found at the end of the book. Chapter 3—Ecosystems: Other

Gibbons, Gail. (1992). *Recycle!: A Handbook for Kids.* Boston: Little, Brown and Company. The process of recycling from start to finish is presented in clear text and detailed watercolor illustrations. Readers also learn about how glass, cans, paper, plastics, and polystyrenes are made. This nonfiction book is a great way to start planning for Earth Day. Chapter 5—Human/Environmental Interaction

Gibbons, Gail. (1995). *Planet Earth/Inside Out.* New York: Morrow Junior Books. Full-page color illustrations and diagrams provide visual information to accompany written descriptions of how scientists believe Earth was formed and how it has changed over billions of years. Descriptions of rocks in the Earth's crust and various "Earth Facts" are found at the end of the book. Chapter 3—Earth's Systems: Nonfiction

Gibbons, Gail. (1999). *Yippee-Yah!: A Book about Cowboys and Cowgirls.* Boston: Little, Brown and Company. In words and detailed watercolor illustrations, Gibbons provides an interesting look at the excitement and adventure of the Old West. This nonfiction book shows clothing, equipment, and the lifestyle of the cowboy. Some famous cowboys and cowgirls as well as historical facts are included. Chapter 4—Westward Expansion

Gibbons, Gail. (2004). *Mummies, Pyramids, and Pharaohs: A Book about Ancient Egypt.* Boston: Little, Brown and Company. Gibbons provides an overview of the life in ancient Egypt. She describes the people, daily activities, beliefs, and customs. Interesting text and detailed watercolor illustrations and diagrams engage the reader. Information about what has been learned from artifacts left behind is also included. Chapter 6—Egypt

Gifted and Talented Students of Pershing Accelerated School. (2001). *We Dream of a World...* New York: Scholastic, Inc. In this *Kids Are Authors* book, 15 students from University City, Missouri, use a template to share their dreams for the world including no hunger, good health, homes, and education for all, where dreams come true... Within each two-page spread, they provide a bright color drawing to match their dream, facts readers should know about that issue, and action readers can undertake to bring about the dream. The last pages of the book provide four blank templates for the readers to create their dreams for the world. Chapter 6—Other

Gilliland, Judith Heide. (2000). *Steamboat!: The Story of Captain Blanche Leathers*. New York: Dorling Kindersley Publishing, Inc. Blanche Leathers wanted to be a steamboat captain from the time she was a young child. She lived along the Mississippi and loved the river. She married a riverboat captain who supported her goal. After much study of the river and a difficult exam, Blanche had to demonstrate her navigational skills. In 1894, Blanche Leathers became the first female steamboat captain. Delightful color illustrations created from cut paper and paint enhance the lively tale of this unique woman. Chapter 4—Transportation: Water

Goodman, Susan E. (2004). *On This Spot: An Expedition Back Through Time*. New York: Greenwillow Books. Goodman has the reader begin on a busy street corner in modern day New York City. Then, turn the page and travel back in time 175 years to a much smaller New York. Another turn and travel to New Amsterdam 350 years ago. The reader continues to move back in time "jumps" until life is just emerging. Dramatic color illustrations complement this unusual text that challenges the reader to think about everything that has happened "on this spot." Although considerably more sophisticated, this book is reminiscent of George Ella Lyon's *Who Came Down That Road?* demonstrating "layers" of history in a given location or object. A timeline is provided at the end of the book. Chapter 6—Layers

Graham, Christine. (1997). *When Pioneer Wagons Rumbled West*. Salt Lake City, Utah: Shadow Mountain. Full-page color illustrations provide a visual backdrop for the simple lyrical text describing the challenges faced by Mormon pioneers heading west. The book includes references to the pioneers' strength of faith. Chapter 4—Westward Expansion

Guiberson, Brenda Z. (1992). *Spoonbill Swamp*. New York: Henry Holt and Company. In storybook fashion, Guilberson describes life in the swamp featuring the activities of spoonbills and alligators. The gentle watercolor illustrations complement this glimpse at the life in the American wetlands. An author's note provides background information about the two animals in this story and the author's concern for the environment in which they live. Chapter 3—Ecosystems: Swamp; Chapter 5—Human/ Environmental Interaction

Guiberson, Brenda Z. (1995). *Winter Wheat*. New York: Henry Holt and Company. While on the surface this appears to be a story about farming, this gently told story about the cycle of winter wheat has greater depth. The flowing text and detailed watercolor illustrations show how farmers and wildlife can share the same piece of land. The author's note provides additional background about the value of the winter wheat growing cycle for humans, migratory birds, and the land. Chapter 3—Ecosystems: Prairie; Chapter 5—Human/Environmental Interaction

Guiberson, Brenda Z. (1998). *Cactus Hotel*. New York: Scholastic, Inc. A day in the Sonoran Desert of southern Arizona is described through the interaction of indigenous animals with their environment and particularly the saguaro cactus. Beautiful detailed watercolors lend visual information to the text as it describes the value of these cacti found only in this one place on Earth. An author's note provides more information about this unique cactus. Chapter 3—Ecosystems: Desert; Chapter 5— Human/Environmental Interaction

Guthrie, Woody. (1998). *This Land Is Your Land*. Boston: Little, Brown and Company. Kathy Jakobsen's detailed paintings illustrate the rich lyrics of a well-loved American folk song. Through her extensive research of Woody Guthrie's life, she was able to feature people and places that were important in his life and travels in the book's illustrations. Some of the lyrics included in the text are seldom heard and make reference to migrant and factory workers who were struggling for better working conditions and higher pay. Readers will enjoy identifying the places included in the illustrations. Chapter 2—Tour the USA: Aesthetic

Hamanaka, Sheila. (1994). *All the Colors of the Earth*. New York: Scholastic, Inc. Full-page color oil paintings complement the simple lyrical text describing the joy in the diversity of all children. Chapter 2—Same and Different Around the World General; Chapter 4—Cultural Mosaics

Harness, Cheryl. (1995). *Three Young Pilgrims*. New York: Aladdin Paperbacks. This book tells the story of one family, the Allertons, who traveled on the Mayflower. Focusing on one year between the autumns of 1620 and 1621, it also tells the story of the whole community. Isaac Allerton and his children, Bartholomew, Remember, and Mary, survived a year of physical and emotional hardship with joy for a future in a new land. After a fictionalized story of the Pilgrim family, Harness introduces the reader to the people, community, and world at that time in history. Detailed, full-page watercolor illustrations complement the story text as well as providing additional information through maps and diagrams. Chapter 4—Immigration

Harness, Cheryl. (1999). *The Amazing Impossible ERIE CANAL*. New York: Aladdin Paperbacks. No one believed a canal connecting the Hudson River to the Great Lakes could be constructed. No one except DeWitt Clinton. His vision resulted in the building of the Erie Canal. In this book Cheryl Harness has presented this unique engineering feat through informative text, detailed maps, and detailed, full-page watercolor illustrations. The maps and diagrams provide additional data about how the canal was built, how the locks work, and specific details of the first trip along the fully completed canal in the fall of 1825. Chapter 5—Construction/Architecture

Hennessy, B. G. (1999). *The Once Upon a Time Map Book: Take a Tour of Six Enchanted Lands*. Cambridge, MA: Candlewick Press. This unique informational book contains beautifully rendered detailed color maps of six famous imaginary lands from fictional favorites including Neverland, Wonderland, and Oz. The reader is encouraged to use his/her map skills to unlock the content of each map. Chapter 1—Creating Maps

High, Linda Oatman. (2001). *Under New York*. New York: Holiday House. With simple text and strong drawings, Oatman shares information about the infrastructure of a unique American city, New York City. A brief informational note at the end of the book expands on some of the content. Chapter 5—Construction/Architecture

High, Linda Oatman. (2004). *City of Snow*. New York: Walker & Company. The Great Blizzard of March 1888 is experienced through the eyes of a young girl whose life in

New York City is disrupted by the record snowfall. Detailed color paintings expand and enhance the free-verse text. The author's note at the end provides the reader with information about how this storm's devastation impacted New York City and the National Weather Service. Chapter 5—Climate/Weather

Hopkinson, Deborah. (2002). *Under the Quilt of Night.* New York: Scholastic, Inc. Rich full-page oil paintings enrich the lyrical text that tells the tale of a young girl and her family as they trust strangers to make their dream of freedom come true. Traveling under the quilt of night, following secret maps and reading signs in quilt patterns, they make their way to Canada via the Underground Railroad, a secret network of people opposed to slavery. Chapter 4—Underground Railroad

Hopkinson, Deborah. (2004). *Apples to Oregon.* New York: An Anne Schwartz Book. Using a tall-tale format, Hopkinson tells the story of how the first apple trees came to Oregon in a wagon in 1847. The oldest daughter, Delicious, describes the exciting challenges she and her family encounter as they move themselves and two wagons loaded with little plants and trees from Salem, Iowa, to Portland, Oregon. The whimsical full-page oil paintings are a perfect accompaniment to the delightful tale. Chapter 4—Westward Expansion

Hopkinson, Deborah. (2006). *Sky Boys: How They Built the Empire State Building.* New York: Schwartz & Wade Books. The Empire State building, one of the most famous buildings in the world, was built during the Great Depression. The story of its construction is told through the eyes of a boy and his father as they watch the world's tallest building (in 1931) as it is constructed, step by step, near their Manhattan home. The text and James Ransome's beautiful oil paintings honor the labor and ingenuity needed to construct this remarkable building. Actual photos of construction workers are on the end papers. Chapter 5—Construction/Architecture

Hiscock, Bruce. (1997). *The Big Rivers: The Missouri, the Mississippi, and the Ohio.* New York: Antheneum Books for Young Readers. This is the story of the incredible flooding in the Midwest in 1993. As he tells the story, Hiscock inserts historical information about the three rivers as well as scientific information that help the reader understand how this devastating flood—one that is only expected every few hundred years—could happen. Detailed watercolor illustrations depict the impact of the flooding on the people and detailed, easy-to-understand diagrams support the scientific content of the book. Chapter 3—Ecosystems: Rivers

Hubbell, Patricia. (2001). *Sea, Sand, Me!* New York: HarperCollins Publishers. The light poetic verse accompanies full-page color illustrations of a day at the beach. This book can be used to provide sensory experiences for young readers and identify the basic characteristics of the beach. Chapter 3—Ecosystems: Other

Jeffers, Susan. (1991). *Brother Eagle, Sister Sky: A Message for Chief Seattle.* New York: Dial Books. Susan Jeffers, the illustrator of this book, has created detailed full-page drawings created with fine-line pen with ink and dyes to accompany the words of Chief Seattle, a respected leader of a Northwestern Indian Nation in the mid 1850s. His words, which have been translated and rewritten more than once, remind the reader that we must care for our environment or risk losing it. Chapter 5—Human/Environmental Interaction

Johnson, Angela. (2007). *wind flyers*. New York: Simon & Schuster Books for Young Readers. A young boy's touching narrative about his uncle's love of flight takes the reader from Alabama to World War II in Europe. The powerful acrylic paintings and lyrical text honor the under-celebrated heroes—the Tuskegee Airmen. Chapter 4—Transportation: Air

Johnston, Tony. (2000). *Desert Song*. San Francisco: Sierra Club Books for Children. The combination of Johnston's lyrical text and Ed Young's rich color paintings of the desert provides a visual and verbal treat for the reader. As the heat of the day fades into night, the nocturnal animals venture out to find food. Then, as the day begins, they go back to sleep until night returns. Chapter 3—Ecosystems: Desert; Chapter 5—Human/Environmental Interaction

Kane, Kristen. (2003). *K Is for Keystone: A Pennsylvania Alphabet*. Chelsea, MI: Sleeping Bear Press. From Easton, the home of the Crayola FACTORY to the Little League baseball fields in Williamsport to the giant steel mills in Pittsburgh, Pennsylvania, has a rich history, variety of geographic features, and many famous residents. Clever poems and informative text reveal the history, geography, and famous people of Pennsylvania. Full-page color paintings accompany the text. Chapter 2—Tasting Places in the USA: Alphabet Books

Karas, G. Brian. (2005). *On Earth*. New York: G. P. Putnam's Sons. This excellent informational book offers simple, yet precise, explanations about Earth's systems—revolution around the sun to create our year, rotation on its axis to create day and night. Colorful, simple full-page paintings illustrate the book's concepts. A brief glossary is included at the end. Chapter 3—Earth's Systems: Nonfiction

Katz, Karen. (1999/2007). *The Colors of Us*. New York: Scholastic, Inc. Lena's skin is the color of cinnamon. Lena's mom who is an artist says that Lena can mix red, yellow, black, and white paints in the right combination to get just the right brown for a picture of herself. Lena doesn't believe it. After all, brown is brown. During walk through the neighborhood meeting friends and family Lena observes that brown isn't just brown. Mr. Pellegrino is the color of pizza crust—golden brown, Sonia is light yellow-brown like creamy peanut butter, Lucy's skin is peachy and tan, and Jo-Jin is the color of honey. Collage, gouache, and colored pencil illustrations demonstrate "the colors of us!" Chapter 2—Same and Different Around the World: General; Chapter 4—Cultural Mosaics

Keller, Laurie. (1998). *The Scrambled States of America*. New York: Scholastic, Inc. Nebraska and Kansas, who are bored, decide to have a party for their fellow 48 states. Two of the states, Virginia and Idaho, announce their plan to trade places for a change of pace. It sounds like a good idea to everyone, so that's just what happens. Alaska moves next to Oklahoma and Kansas goes to Hawaii's usual location in the Pacific. Keller's clever dialog and whimsical color illustrations provide a clever way to explain the significance of location. Chapter 2—Tasting Places in the USA; Chapter 3—Earth's Systems: Fiction

Kent, Peter. (1998). *Hidden Under the Ground: The World Beneath Your Feet.* New York: Dutton Children's Books. This intriguing nonfiction book offers a wide range of information about "the world beneath your feet." Fascinating two-page spreads offer facts and detailed drawings organized around 12 themes including Caves and Caverns, Homes, and Traveling Underground. Additional information provides an overall look at using the underground, "subterranean celebrities, and a glossary." Chapter 5—Construction/Architecture

Kinkade, Sheila. (2006). *My Family.* Watertown, MA: Charlesbridge. A collage of color photographs document the variety of shapes and sizes families come in all around the world. The text identifies the commonalities of families as they live, learn, work, and play together. A portion of the proceeds from the book are donated to the Global Fund for Children to support community-based educational programs around the world. Chapter 2—Same and Different Around the World: General

Knight, Margy Burns. (1992). *Talking Walls.* Gardiner, ME: Tilbury House. This book describes walls located in different countries around the world, from the Great Wall of China to the Berlin Wall, and discusses their significance. The author places children of the past and present at these sites, showing the effect each wall has on them. Large, full-color paintings illustrate each wall. The end of the book has an informative paragraph about each of the 14 walls found in the book. Each wall is located on a world map. Chapter 6—Lesson Plan 6.3

Kratter, Paul. (2004). *The Living Rain Forest: An Animal Alphabet.* Watertown, MA: Charlesbridge. Rainforests, threatened by deforestation, global warming, and over-hunting, contain over half the earth's animal species. Paul Kratter shares an alphabet of animals found in the rainforest. Some are familiar, others very rare. Lovely acrylic and watercolor illustrations accompany brief descriptive paragraphs about of the 26 animals. Animal sizes, behaviors, coloration, habitat, and diet are included. A world map on the end papers identify the locations of the animals found in the book. Chapter 3—Ecosystems: Rain Forest

Kurtz, Jane. (2000). *Faraway Home.* San Diego: Gulliver Books. Beautiful full-page watercolor illustrations enrich the story of young Desta who worries as her father prepares to visit his homeland of Ethiopia. Desta, who has only known life in America, is concerned that her father, who shares his love of Ethiopia with her, might want to chose to stay when he returns. As the book ends, Desta realizes that her father can love both homelands. Chapter 4—Immigration

Lasky, Kathryn. (2006). *John Muir: America's First Environmentalist.* Cambridge, MA: Candlewick Press. Exquisite acrylic paintings depict John Muir's life as well as the American wilderness he loved. This beautiful biography, organized by chapters, shares the events and accomplishments of John's life, as well as his love of the land. John Muir was influential in establishing one of the first national parks in America,

Yosemite. He also founded the Sierra Club conservation group. Additional information about readings and the Sierra Club are included at the end of the book. Chapter 5—Human/Environmental Interaction

Lee, Millie. (2006). *Landed.* New York: Frances Foster Books. Based on the true story of the author's father-in-law, 12-year-old Sun leaves southeast China to joint his father in San Francisco. Unfortunately he is held and interrogated at Angel Island. The book alternates a full page of text with a full-page color illustration. The text is enhanced by the detailed, yet softly colored illustrations. Chapter 4—Immigration

Leedy, Loreen. (2000). *Mapping Penny's World.* New York: Scholastic, Inc. Lisa and her class are Creating Maps this month in school. She uses the skills she's learning at school to map her dog, Penny's, world. Lisa, with Penny's help, creates a map of her bedroom, a treasure map of the back yard that has a map key and a map of her hiking trails using a scale to show the real distances. The full-page color illustrations were created by combining digital painting and photo collage in Adobe Photoshop. Chapter 1—Creating Maps

Lewin, Ted. (1996). *Market!* New York: HarperCollins Publishers. Beautiful full-page watercolor illustrations filled with people and action join simple text to compare and contrast markets around the world: Equador, Nepal, Ireland, United States, and Morocco. The site and content of the markets may differ, but the need to buy and sell is common to all. Chapter 4—Cultural Mosaics: Other

Lewin, Ted. (2001). *Red Legs: A Drummer Boy of the Civil War.* New York: HarperCollins Publisher. Cleverly described in text and beautiful full-page color paintings, Lewin tells the story of life as a drummer boy in the Civil War. Based on the life of Stephen Benjamin Bartow in the 14th Regiment, Company E, a unit from Brooklyn, New York, the story in Lewin's book turns out to be a reenactment. In this story Stephen dies, but in real life he lived until 1911 at age 65. Stephen was a mason who helped build the Brooklyn Bridge. Chapter 4—Civil War

Lewin, Ted. (2003). *Lost City: The Discovery of Machu Picchu.* New York: Philomel Books. The lives of a young Quechua boy and Yale professor Hiram Bingham cross in the mountains of Peru in July 1911. This fictional telling of the historic discovery of Machu Picchu is beautifully illustrated with full-page watercolor paintings. Lewin, who followed Bingham's footsteps in order to experience the adventure he had read about in Bingham's journal, recounts the story through the thoughts of both the boy and Bingham. A note at the end of the book describes the excavation of Machu Picchu. Chapter 4—Exploration

Lin, Grace, and McKneally, Ranida T. (2006). *Our Seasons.* New York: Charlesbridge. Four children, Ki-Ki, Owen, Lily, and Kevin, experience the seasons of the year in this delightful book. Lin's evocative haiku and charming color illustrations teamed with McKneally's season-related questions and answers provide a great wealth of information about the seasons and how they affect weather, the natural world, and the human body. A brief glossary is included at the end of the book. Chapter 3—Earth's Systems: Nonfiction

Logan, Claudia (2004). *The 5,000-Year-Old Puzzle: Solving a Mystery of Ancient Egypt.* New York: Scholastic, Inc. Young Will Hunt and his family are joining an archaeological expedition to Giza in 1924. Dr. George Reisner will lead the expedition. Will's journal entries from mid-November 1924 to mid-June 1927 share the excitement and frustration, as well as joy in archaeological discovery. The acrylic and watercolor illustrations include landscapes, maps, diagrams, postcards—you name it—that enrich the journal entries. Additional information is found in factual reports and photos from Dr. Reisner's expedition. Dr. Reisner was the first to use systematic excavations in Egypt and use photographic documentation. Will and his family are fictional, but the rest of the story is based on actual records. Chapter 6—Egypt

Loomis, Christine. (2000). *Across America, I Love You.* New York: Hyperion Books for Children. In this unique serenade to her child, Loomis uses lyrical text to describe the beauties of various locales around the United States from the Alaskan wilds to the Midwestern heartland to the Florida Everglades. Accompanied by full-page oil paintings of the land and small thumbnails of her growing daughter, the text expresses love for both country and child. Chapter 2—Tour the USA: Aesthetic

Lorenz, Albert with Schleh, Joy. (2003). *Journey to Cahokia: A Young Boy's Visit to the Great Mound City.* New York: Harry N. Abrams, Inc. Little Hawk and his family take a trip from their village near Lake Erie on the Sandusky River in current day Ohio to Cahokia, the great mound city near current day St. Louis on the Mississippi. Set in 1200 C.E., this story based on new research and illustrated with historically accurate drawings, tells about a family's long journey to this Native American urban center. Along the way the reader learns more about the rich culture of this thriving culture. An introductory detailed map, archival photos, and the author's note support the story text. Chapter 4—Cultural Mosaic: Native American

Lyon, George Ella. (2000). *One Lucky Girl.* New York: Dorling Kindersley Publishing, Inc. On a Sunday afternoon, about four o'clock, Hawkeye and his parents were sitting in the shade outside their trailer at the racetrack. His baby sister, Becky, was taking a nap in the trailer. The family, seeing the tornado, "hit the dirt." When the tornado had passed and the family stood to assess the damage, they discovered their trailer—and Becky—were gone! Based on a true story, full-page color pastel illustrations enhance the discovery of Becky who miraculously slept through the tornado that carried her into the field in the center of the racetrack. Chapter 3—Earth's Systems: Fiction; Chapter 5—Climate/Weather

Macaulay, David. (1997). *Rome Antics.* Boston: Houghton Mifflin Company. "Somewhere in the Italian hills, a homing pigeon is released. She soars quickly and follows an old road, which (of course) leads to Rome." Thus begins the unique tour through the city of Rome. Zooming through the landscape, viewing people and places from a variety of vantages, the reader sees Rome through the pigeon's eye. Macaulay's signature black-and-white drawings include the ancient and the modern. A map of the city "as the pigeon flies" and descriptive paragraphs describing historic landmarks complete the book. Chapter 6—Layers

Maestro, Betsy. (1996). *Coming to America: The Story of Immigration.* New York: Scholastic, Inc. America is a nation of immigrants. This book explores the long history of people coming for a multitude of reasons from the nomads who crossed the land bridge from Asia to current day Alaska to later people who came looking for religious and political freedom. The interesting narrative that explains our rich diversity is accompanied by detailed watercolor illustrations. Chapter 4—Immigration

McCann, Michelle R. (2003). *Luba: The Angel of Bergen-Belsen.* Berkley, CA: Tricycle Press. One cold December night in 1944, Luba Tryszynska found 54 children abandoned behind the concentration camp at Bergen-Belson. Through her monumental efforts and those of the women in her barracks, the children all survived until their release by the British in April 1945. Riveting text and dramatic oil and collage illustrations tell this true story. The author provides an epilogue and additional information at the end of the book. Certainly a difficult story for young children, but a wonderful background story for teachers. Chapter 4—World War II: Europe

McDonald, Megan. (2005). *Saving the Liberty Bell.* New York: A Richard Jackson Book. Eleven-year-old John Jacob Mickley and his father have an exciting adventure as they assist in saving the Liberty Bell from the British. Hiding the bell under the mound of straw, potato sacks, and a lady's hoop skirt, they transported it from Philadelphia to Bethlehem. Whimsical acrylic paintings match the tall tale telling of this historic event. Chapter 4—Revolutionary War

McDonald, Suse. (1995). *Nanta's Lion.* New York: Morrow Junior Books. In her Maasai village, Nanta wants to see the lion her father and other hunters are seeking. Nanta goes off on her own to find the lion. Although she sees a variety of native animals, Nanta is frustrated because she cannot find the lion. Exquisite color landscapes change as the reader turns die-cut pages to reveal the lion Nanta never sees in this fantasy! Chapter 2—Africa

Melmed, Laura Krauss. (2001). *This First Thanksgiving Day: A Counting Story.* New York: HaperCollins Publisher. Using simple rhymes and a counting theme from 1 to 12, young Wampanoag and Pilgrim children are shown engaged in their chores that lead to the first Thanksgiving. Colorful, detailed paintings provide hidden surprises for children to find. Chapter 4—Immigration

Melmed, Laura Krauss. (2003). *Capital!: Washington D.C. from A to Z.* New York: HarperCollins Publishers. Rhyming verses and informative text engage the reader in a rich tour of our nation's capital. Important buildings, memorials, locations, and people are highlighted in this lively excursion through a unique city. Colorful paintings enhance the text. A map on the endpapers and flyleafs provide locations for the 26 stops along the tour. Chapter 2—Tasting Places in the USA: Alphabet Books

Millard, Anne. (1998). *A Street Through Time*. London: Dorling Kindersley Ltd. This beautiful book follows the life of a street through thousands years from 10,000 B.C.E. When Stone Age hunters used this place as a winter camp along side a river to its current status as a busy street in an urban setting. The detailed full-page color illustrations in this oversized book carry most of the information about change over time. Limited, factual text accompanies the 14 key periods in history documented by the illustrations. Chapter 6—Layers

Mollel, Tololwa M. (1999). *My Rows and Piles of Coins*. New York: Clarion Books. Saruni has been working to earn enough money to buy a bicycle so that he can help his parents carry goods to market in his native Tanzania. He continues to save the money as he learns to ride his father's bike. When the day comes to purchase his own bike, he doesn't have enough money! Despite his disappointment, the problem is resolved. Striking watercolor paintings capture the bright daylight of the Tanzanian marketplace and the happy interactions of Saruni's family. Chapter 2—Same and Different Around the World: Africa

Montanari, Donata. (2001). *Children Around the World*. Toronto, ON: Kids Can Press Ltd. Twelve fictional children briefly describe their lives in their home countries. Each child shares information about family, play, school, and country. The colorful multimedia collages create unique children in each locale. The simple text and pictures explore the themes of commonality and diversity. Chapter 2—Same and Different Around the World: General

Morley, Jacqueline. (2002). *You Wouldn't Want to Be an American Pioneer!: A Wilderness You'd Rather Not Tame*. New York: Franklin Watts. Cartoon-like detailed color illustrations and a somewhat irreverently written text is sure to delight young readers of this nonfiction book about the challenges and reasons so many took on the dangers of both a journey across the vast country and settling in a new region. The information is organized by topics with clever titles like "Mealtimes—Feeling Queasy?" and presented on two-page spreads. A glossary and index are included. This is part of a series of books. Chapter 4—Westward Expansion

Morpurgo, Michael. (2000). *Wombat Goes Walkabout*. Cambridge, MA: Candlewick Press. Reminiscent of the classic *Are You My Mother?*, Wombat awakens from a nap in his burrow thinking about why he's a wombat and discovers his mother is missing. As he travels through the outback to find her, he encounters other native creatures including Kookaburra, Wallaby, Possum, and Boy who show him what they can do. None of them think Wombat's digging is special until danger threatens the Bush. Soft-edged color illustrations complement this informational fantasy. Chapter 3—Ecosystems: Rivers

Moss, Marissa. (1999). *True Heart*. San Diego: Silver Whistle. Inspired by a vintage photo she saw at the California State Railroad Museum, Moss tells the story of young Bee who has dreamed of becoming an engineer since she was 16. Set in the late

1800s, Bee tells the story of how she worked to support her family and pursue her dream to become an engineer. Striking full-page color photos support Bee's narration. Chapter 4—Transportation: Land

Munro, Roxie. (2001). *The Inside-Outside Book of Texas*. New York: Sea Star Book. Detailed ink and watercolor drawings take the reader on a journey through the big state of Texas from the skyscrapers of Dallas to the rustic southwestern border. Simple labels on each drawing aid the reader in finding the locations on a map at the end of the book. Informational paragraphs about each location are also included. Chapter 2—Tasting Places in the USA

Musgrove, Margaret. (1992). *Ashanti to Zulu*. New York: Puffin Books. This collection of vignettes, accompanied by detailed color drawing, introduces the reader to 26 African tribes through the depiction of a custom important to each. The 1977 Caldecott winner continues to be a valuable book to use in the study of Africa. The 26 tribes are located on an African map at the end of the book. Chapter 2—Same and Different Around the World: Africa

Nelson, Vaunda Micheaux. (2003). *Almost to Freedom*. New York: Scholastic, Inc. Sally tells the story of her life as the rag doll loved by a young slave and her family. Inspired by a rag doll found in an Underground Railroad hideout, Nelson's fictional story describes the hardships of slavery and the dangers associated with the journey. Chapter 4—Underground Railroad

Noble, Trinka Hakes. (2004). *The Scarlet Stockings Spy*. Chelsea, MI: Sleeping Bear Press. Young Maddy Rose helps her mother and works in Mistress Ross's Upholstery Shop in Philadelphia. Each week she secretly helps her brother, Jonathan, positioned with Washington's army. Her small clothesline, hung from her third-floor window, holds their secret code for the ships at anchor in the harbor. This poignant story, set in 1777, demonstrates that even the smallest of citizens can be patriots in time of war. Full-page, softly colored detailed illustrations visually set the story. Chapter 4—Revolutionary War

Noble, Trinka Hakes. (2005). *One for All: A Pennsylvania Number Book*. Chelsea, MI: Sleeping Bear Press. Using numbers in sequence 1 to 20 and then in tens from 30 to 100, Noble invites the reader to count all the wonderful symbols, landmarks, events, and people who make Pennsylvania great. Clever rhymes introduce the numbers while instructive paragraphs provide further information. Softly colored full-page illustrations complement the text. This book is an excellent companion to *K Is for Keystone* by Kristen Kane. Chapter 2—Tasting Places in the USA: Alphabet Books

Noble, Trinka Hakes. (2006). *The Last Brother: A Civil War Tale*. Chelsea, MI: Sleeping Bear Press. Eleven-year-old Gabe enlists in the Union Army in Pennsylvania as a bugler with his older brother, Davy. Just before his first battle, Gabe goes into the woods for quiet and meets another young bugler, a Confederate boy. Soon the quiet ends and Gabe's first battle, the Battle of Gettysburg, begins. Gabe's desire to protect his brother leads him to a heroic act. Beautiful realistic full-page color illustrations capture the drama and emotion of the story. Chapter 4—Civil War

Noguchi, Rick and Jenks, Deneen. (2001). *Flowers from Mariko*. New York: Lee & Low Books, Inc. Mariko and her family are released from a Japanese American internment camp after spending three years there. Mariko doesn't fully understand why they were forced to be in the camp, but she does understand that returning to the outside world won't be easy. While they wait for Father, a gardener before the war, to find work they live in yet another camp along with other Japanese Americans. Mariko plants a garden in hopes of lifting everyone's spirit. This heart-warming story and the uniquely created illustrations portray the difficulties and injustices endured by Japanese Americans through the eyes of a young girl. Chapter 4—World War II: Japanese-American Internment Camps

O'Brien, Patrick. (2000). *Steam, Smoke, and Steel: Back in Time with Trains*. New York: Charlesbridge Publishing. A young boy narrates the story of his family and their experiences with trains from the 1830s when his great-great-great-great-grandfather began the engineering tradition. Each generation is introduced by a detailed watercolor and gouache painting of a train of that era. The text provides facts and anecdotes about trains and the people who drive them in a lovely conversational style. Chapter 4—Transportation: Land

Olaleye, Isaac. (2001). *Bikes for Rent!* New York: Orchard Books. Lateef wants to rent a bicycle from the bicycle stall in his village in western Nigeria. So he works very hard collecting firewood and mushrooms in the rainforest. Finally he earns enough to rent a bike and ride with his friends. But all does not go well as he tries to rent and ride an even bigger bike! Simple watercolor drawings capture the adventures and enthusiasm of Lateef as he learns about responsibility while he strives to be included. Chapter 2—Same and Different Around the World: Africa

Onyefulu, Ifeoma. (1996). *OGBO: Sharing Life in an African Village*. New York: Gulliver Books. Seven-year-old Obioma (o-bee-O-ma), a young Nigerian girl, helps the reader understand the age-old African tradition of belonging to an *ogbo* or age group. Beautiful color photographs and the first person narrative introduces the reader to Obioma's family member and their *ogbo*'s accomplishments that help create the fabric of village life. Chapter 2—Same and Different Around the World: Africa

Onyefulu, Ifeoma. (1997). *A Is for Africa*. New York: A Puffin Unicorn. The photographs, taken in Nigeria, reflect the rich diversity of the African continent. The author notes that her purpose in writing this alphabet book was to capture what the people of Africa have in common: traditional village life, warm family ties, and hospitality. Beautiful color photographs with clearly written informational paragraphs open the African continent to the reader. Chapter 2—Same and Different Around the World: Africa

Otto, Carolyn. (1999). *Pioneer Church*. New York: Henry Holt and Company. With a focus on the community church, Otto tells the story of growth and change in a community from its beginnings in pre-Revolutionary Pennsylvania through the Civil War and into modern times. Although the congregation moved from the old church on the hill to more modern facilities with electricity and water, the old church became a historic landmark and continues to be part of the community. Based on the history of Old Zion Church in Brickerville, Pennsylvania, the story and detailed oil paintings tell a story common across the country. Chapter 6—Layers

Pallotta, Jerry. (1994). *The Spice Alphabet Book.* Watertown, MA: Charlesbridge. Colorful, detailed illustrations provide a perfect backdrop for each of the herbs, spices, and other natural flavors discussed in this unique alphabet book. The informative paragraphs are enhanced and expanded by visual information in the illustrations. The artist's notes at the end of the book offers additional facts. Chapter 4—Cultural Mosaics

Pallotta, Jerry, and Stillwell, Fred. (1997). *The Airplane Alphabet Book.* Watertown, MA: Charlesbridge. Extraordinary full-color realistic illustrations of airplanes from the Wright brothers' first flying machine to the modern Ultralight document the history of flying. The easy-to-read, yet information-packed, paragraphs take the reader on an amazing trip through one of humankind's greatest achievement. Chapter 4—Transportation: Air

Park, Frances, and Park, Ginger. (2002). *Good-bye, 382 Shin Dang Dong.* Washington, D.C.: National Geographic Society. Jangmi is sad because she is leaving Korea to go to America; 382 Shin Dang Dong is the address of the house she is leaving. Rich oil paintings reflect the concerns the young girl expresses as she thinks about all she is leaving. Through the support and excitement of her parents, however, she begins to enjoy the prospect of life in her new home at 112 Foster Terrace, Brighton, Massachusetts, U.S.A. Chapter 4—Immigration

Peacock, Louise. (1998). *Crossing the Delaware: A History in Many Voices.* New York: Scholastic, Inc. Fictional letters exchanged by Harry who is serving in the pre-Revolutionary War militia and his girlfriend, Jenny, tell the personal story of this historic event. Also included is an informational narrative by the author that expands the content of Harry's letters. Other voices lending drama and information to this unique telling are offered through quotations from Washington, some of his officers and soldiers who served with him. Color illustrations and other historic art add visual details. Chapter 4—Revolutionary War

Perez, Amada Irma. (2002). *My Diary from Here to There.* San Francisco: Children's Book Press. This delightful book, written in Spanish and English, is an autobiographical retelling of the author's experience immigrating to the United States from Mexico. Questions fill the diary entries that carry the story of excitement and fear in making such a huge life change. The charming narrative and bold color illustrations are perfect for readers of all ages. Chapter 4—Immigration

Pinkney, Sandra L. (2000). *Shades of Black: A Celebration of Our Children.* New York: Scholastic, Inc. Children's faces, "in shades of black," smile out of the photographs in this celebration of diversity within unity. Simple text and color photos set on pages of various shades of brown identify the beauty in the variety of skin tones, hair texture, and eye color of black children. Chapter 2—Same and Different Around the World: General; Chapter 4—Cultural Mosaics

Polacco, Patricia. (1995). *Pink and Say.* New York: Scholastic, Inc. Sheldon Russell Curtis, "Say," was wounded in a fierce battle in Georgia during the Civil War. Pinkus "Pink" Aylee, a black Union soldier, found him and took him home to be nursed back to health. On their way back to their own companies, the two teens were captured by the Confederates and taken to the Andersonville prison. This true story has been passed from great-grandfather to grandmother to son and finally to the author-artist, who passes it on to the reader and dedicates it to the memory of Pinkus Aylee. Chapter 4—Civil War

Polacco, Patricia. (2000). *The Butterfly.* New York: Scholastic, Inc. Patricia Polacco shares another dramatic and heartwarming family story in this book. Her aunt, Monique, was a child in France during the Nazi occupation. This book tells of a brave and dangerous event in the young girl's life when she discovers her mother is part of the French underground providing a safe haven for Jews escaping the Nazis. Detailed color illustrations portray the emotions of Monique, her mother, and other characters in this moving story. Chapter 4—World War II: Europe

Polacco, Patricia. (2004). *An Orange for Frankie.* New York: Philomel Books. Set in turn-of-the-century rural Michigan, Frankie and his family are waiting for Pa to return from Lansing where he has driven his horse and wagon to meet the train from Florida to collect nine oranges for the family's Christmas Eve tradition. Polacco's signature paintings extend the text as she shares another piece of family history that reveals the joys of family and the unique life in this region of rural America. Chapter 4—Transportation: Land

Poole, Josephine. (2005). *Anne Frank.* New York: Alfred A. Knopf. Poole offers a compelling biography of Anne Frank that provides the reader with background about the young girl before she and her family had to hide from the Nazis. Beautifully detailed illustrations are haunting complements to the poignant text that tells one girl's story that has affected millions of people. Chapter 4—World War II: Europe

Priceman, Marjorie. (2005). *Hot Air: The (Mostly) True Story of the First Hot-Air Balloon Ride.* New York: Atheneum Books for Young Readers. The setting is the Palace of Versailles on September 19, 1783, the event is the demonstration of an exciting new kind of transportation, and the passengers are a duck, a sheep, and a rooster! Although the reader is sure to believe this is a fantasy—and it is—the story of the first hot-air balloon demonstration actually carried barnyard animals. Full-color, whimsical illustrations are a perfect complement to the text. A brief description of the year leading up to the historic demonstration is included. Chapter 4—Transportation: Air

Provensen, Alice. (2005). *Klondike Gold.* New York: Simon & Schuster Books for Young Readers. Before she tells this story, Provensen introduces the reader to the setting through a formal introduction and map of the route from Seattle to St. Michael, Alaska. Then she offers the adventure of prospecting for gold based on the true story of Bill Howell one of the brave prospectors looking for gold in 1897. The verbal and visual telling of the story is organized in a unique triptych format. The top half of each two-page spread holds a detailed oil painting and the bottom quarter hold informational text and/or diagrams and illustrations while the middle quarter carries the story narrative. Chapter 4—Westward Expansion; Exploration

Ransom, Candice. (2003). *Liberty Street*. New York: Walker & Company. Young Kezia is a slave living in pre-Civil War Fredericksburg, Virginia. She's learning to read, an illegal act, but commits another one as she escapes Fredericksburg to travel on the Underground Railroad to Canada. Beautiful oil paintings complement the text. Most of the stories describing slavery and the Underground Railroad are set on plantations. This story, set in a city, reminds the readers that slaves also worked in smaller households. Chapter 4—Underground Railroad

Raven, Margot Theis. (2004). *Circle Unbroken: The Story of a Basket and Its People*. New York: Melanie Kroupa Books. Grandma teaches her young granddaughter the intricate art of sewing sweetgrass baskets as she relates the story of how this craft was carried from Africa and passed down through generations. Set in the Lowcountry, this story and craft are specific to the Gullah (South Carolina) or Geechee (Georgia) culture that was brought to the Sea Island plantations. Many of the descendents of the slaves live there today and create the coveted sweetgrass baskets. Beautiful full-page color illustrations complement the text. Chapter 4—Cultural Mosaics

Reynolds, Marilynn. (1999). *The Prairie Fire*. Victoria, BC Canada: Orca Book Publishers. Set in the prairie provinces of Canada, this book tells the universal story of survival of prairie fires in North America. Young Percy is in a hurry to grow up and participate in heavy chores. Despite his age, he joins his parents in saving their homestead from the devastating prairie fire. Detailed color pencil drawings provide visual drama to the story's text. Chapter 3—Ecosystems: Prairie

Ringgold, Faith. (1995). *Aunt Harriet's Underground Railroad in the Sky*. New York: Crown. Fictional characters Cassie and her brother, Be Be, encounter historical figure Harriet Tubman as they soar through the skies. Within this fantasy adventure, the author shares information about the Underground Railroad and Harriet Tubman's life. Rich, full-page, color paintings enhance the text. The author provides a biographical profile of Tubman at the end of the book along with a map of the Underground Railroad routes and sources for further reading. Chapter 4—Underground Railroad

Root, Phyllis. (2004). *If You Want to See a Caribou*. Boston: Houghton Mifflin Co. Through lyrical text the author reveals the wonders of nature on an island in Lake Superior. Rich, detailed color woodcut prints complement the text. Chapter 3—Ecosystems: Rivers

Rumford, James. (2001). *Traveling Man: The Journey of Ibn Battuta, 1325–1354*. Boston: Houghton Mifflin Company. The story of a traveler in the fourteenth century before Columbus when many believed the world was flat. Like Marco Polo, Ibn Battuta left an account of his incredible journey from Morocco to China to the steppes of Russia to shore of Tanzania—75,000 miles in all. Stylized pictures, maps, and journal entries take the reader on the remarkable journey. Included is a glossary explaining more about the people, places, and things discussed in the text. Also a map of the travels is included. Chapter 4—Exploration

Russo, Marisabina. (2005). *Always Remember Me: How One Family Survived World War II*. New York: An Anne Schwartz Book. Young Rachel loves Sundays when she comes to Oma's (Grandmother's) house for the weekly dinner. Oma has two picture albums. One shows happy times from after World War II when she and her daughters had come to America. The other album, about the sad part of Oma's life, has always remained closed. But today Oma shares the story of her family's survival. This is a warm, easily understood story of the war drama. Reproductions of family photographs line the endpapers like an album while gouache illustrations, imitating photographs, accompany the true story of the author's family history. Chapter 4—World War II

Rylant, Cynthia. (1998). *Tulip Sees America*. New York: The Blue Sky Press. A young man grows up in Ohio without ever seeing other places. As soon as he's old enough, he decides to buy a car and drive all the way to Oregon. He and his dog, Tulip, climb into their new green Beetle and drive west through Iowa, Nebraska, Wyoming, Colorado, Nevada, and then Oregon. In each state they identify the most outstanding feature. Full-page unique oil paintings perfectly match the simple text with a powerful message. Chapter 2—Tour the USA: Aesthetic

St. George, Judith. (2005). *So You Want to Be an Explorer?* New York: Philomel Books. Whimsical color drawings and witty text set the tone of this celebration of explorers big and small. Organized by the characteristics explorers need or experience, the narrative text groups dozens of well-known explorers like Amelia Earhart, Amerigo Vespucci, and Edmund Hillary or lesser names such as Barbara Washburn and Hugo Eckener. A glossary of the explorers is furnished at the end of the book. Chapter 4—Exploration

Saul, Carol P. (1995). *Someplace Else*. New York: Simon & Schuster Books for Young Readers. After spending her whole life by an apple orchard, Mrs. Tillby leaves her son to run the orchard as she searches for someplace else to live. As she visits her other children who live in a city, in the mountains, and at the shore, she loves each one, but not enough to stay permanently. The full-page color illustrations and lively text carry the reader to someplace else and Mrs. Tilly's clever solution to her dilemma. Chapter 3—Ecosystems: Rivers

Say, Allen. (2005). *Kamishibai Man*. Boston: Houghton Mifflin Company. An old kamishibai man, a storyteller from Japan's recent past, decides to return to the city where he once shared his stories and candies with the children before the advent of television. Although the city is vastly different from what he remembers, he finds the adults who were once his young audience anxious to rehear his stories and taste his candies. Say's detailed color illustrations are a gentle visual treat accompanying this lovely story. Chapter 2—Same and Different Around the World: Asia

Schaefer, Lola M. (2006). *An Island Grows*. New York: Greenwillow Books. Simple, precise rhymes describe the birth of an island under the sea and follow its development to land that sustain human, plant, and animal life. Colorful paper collage illustrations support and enhance the verse. Scientific details about how volcanic islands grow appear at the end of the book. Chapter 3—Earth's Systems: Nonfiction

Schanzer, Rosalyn. (1997). *How We Crossed the West: The Adventures of Lewis and Clark.* New York: Scholastic, Inc. Thomas Jefferson and the Congress asked Meriwether Lewis who asked William Clark to join him in an extraordinary mission to explore the western rivers all the way to the western ocean, meet and begin trading with Indian tribes, discover new plants and animals, and make new maps. Schanzer relates the remarkable two-and-a-half-year journey through student-friendly journal entries and illustrations rendered in the quaint painting style of American folk artists of the period. A map in the front and back of the book provides the route from St. Louis to the mouth of the Columbia River at the Pacific. Chapter 4—Exploration

Schanzer, Rosalyn. (2000). *Escaping to America: A True Story.* New York: HarperCollins Publishers. The author relates the story of her family's immigration from Poland to the United States in 1921 to escape the war. Schanzer describes the complicated process and stresses of the preparation and journey. Detailed color illustrations complement the text. Some illustrations are based on family photographs. Chapter 4—Immigration

Schonberg, Marcia. (2000). *B Is for Buckeye.* Chelsea, MI: Sleeping Bear Press. From John Glenn, the first astronaut to circle Earth, to the Wright brothers who invented an airplane that would fly, to James Murray Spangler who patented an electric suction sweeper, to Shawnee Chief Tecumseh, Ohio is home to many famous residents. This book uses clever poems and informative text to reveal the rich history, geography, and famous people of the state called "The Mother of Presidents." Full-page color paintings accompany the text. Chapter 2—Tasting Places in the USA: Alphabet Books

Scillian, Devin. (2001). *A Is for America.* Chelsea, MI: Sleeping Bear Press. This alphabet book pays tribute to the features we know and love about our country. Poems provide a brief taste of each stop and expository text broadens the reader's background knowledge. Colorful detailed illustrations enhance the entries about people such as James Monroe, places like Kitty Hawk, and events including the gold rush that represent the United States of America. Chapter 2—Tour the USA: Aesthetic

Seuling, Barbara. (1998/2002). *Winter Lullaby.* San Diego: Browndeer Press. *Winter Lullaby* answers questions young children ask about animals as winter approaches: "When the breeze blows the petals off the flowers, where do the bees go?" Beautiful full-page acrylic paintings identify a variety of locations as the context for both questions and answers including the plains, the desert, and the mountains. Chapter 3—Earth's Systems: Fiction

Seuling, Barbara. (2001). *Spring Song.* San Diego: Gulliver Books. With simple, but provocative questions, this book takes a unique look at the signs of spring. Beautiful full-page acrylic paintings offer details to expand the text and encourage young readers to consider nature's celebration of a new season. Chapter 3—Earth's Systems: Fiction

Siebert, Diane. (2000). *Cave.* New York: HarperCollins Publishers. Through her signature lyrical text, Siebert describes the physical and historical characteristics of caves. The striking acrylic paintings present the world of the cave from unusual perspectives within the cave. An author's note and pronunciation guide is provided. Chapter 3—Ecosystems: Rivers; Chapter 5—Human/Environmental Interaction

Siebert, Diane. (2001). *Mississippi.* New York: HarperCollins Publishers. Through her signature lyrical text, Siebert describes the rich history and beauty of the Mississippi from before humans sought its riches. Beautiful full-color illustrations complement the text. River words are defined in a glossary at the end. End papers provide a complete map of the Mississippi from its origin in Minnesota to its delta entry in the Gulf of Mexico. Chapter 3—Ecosystems: Rivers

Siebert, Diane. (2006). *Tour America: A Journey Through Poems and Art.* San Francisco: Chronicle Books. Diane Siebert and her husband toured the United States on motorcycles, mostly camping, for 10 years. Every evening she wrote in her journal and those writings have generated children's books and articles for magazines. This book is a collection of poems inspired by these experiences, illustrated in a variety of media to match the poetic vision of Siebert and the illustrator's own experiences. A map at the beginning of the book identifies the 26 locations that inspired the work. An informational box on each page offers factual information to complement the poetry and art. Chapter 2—Tour the USA: Aesthetic

Simon, Seymour. (2000). *Seymour Simon's Book of Trucks.* New York: Simon & Schuster Books for Young Readers. Inspired by his grandchildren's fascination with all kinds of vehicles, Simon wrote this book about trucks. Simple factual text and full-page color photos provide verbal and visual information about more than a dozen trucks. Chapter 4—Transportation: Land

Smith, David J. (2002). *If the World Were a Village: A Book about the World's People.* Toronto, ON: Kids Can Press. In the introduction, Smith suggests we imagine the whole world's population as a village of just 100 people before we examine their characteristics. That means each person in the village would represent 62 million from the real world. The book is organized by 11 descriptors including nationalities, languages, religions, money and possessions, schooling and literacy, and electricity. Full-page color paintings illustrate the global village. Smith, a strong advocate of teaching our children about the global village, offers some suggestions for doing so at the end of this interesting and surprising book. Chapter 4—Cultural Mosaic

Sobel, June. (2003). *B Is for Bulldozer: A Construction ABC.* San Diego: Gulliver Books. This clever rhyming story tells about all the construction vehicles, tools, and materials needed to build an amusement park. The simple rhyme using vocabulary beginning with each letter of the alphabet is enhanced by colorful acrylic paintings of each identified item—perfect for young children. Chapter 5—Construction/Architecture

Solheim, James. (1999). *It's Disgusting—And We Ate It!: True Food Facts from Around the World—and Throughout History!* New York: Scholastic, Inc. Clever cartoon drawings created with colored pencils and acrylic paints are a perfect match to the tone of this charming book about what many might consider unconventional food. What students wouldn't simulate gagging as they listen closely to a reading of humorous entries describing the bizarre foods humans have eaten and *loved* over time. Organized into three parts, this unusual, but fascinating book provides the reader with plenty of "food for thought." Sorry, I just couldn't resist! Chapter 4—Cultural Mosaics: Other

Stevenson, Harvey. (2005). *Looking at Liberty.* New York: HarperCollins Publisher. As an American living in France, Stevenson was inspired to write the story of Lady Liberty. With poignant lyrical verse and muted colors, Stevenson's text and uniquely composed full-page paintings are dramatic. Brief explanatory paragraphs are included at various points and a detailed timeline appears at the end of the book. Chapter 2—Tasting Places in the USA

Stroud, Bettye. (2005). *The Patchwork Path: A Quilt Map to Freedom.* Cambridge, MA: Candlewick Press. Ten-year-old Hannah is a slave on a Georgia plantation. Her mother taught her the code contained within quilt squares that will help guide her to freedom. After her sister, Mary, is sold to another far-off plantation and her mother dies, Hannah and her father have the opportunity to escape to Canada. Along the way, Hannah thinks about the code her mother taught her and how it helps them find freedom. Beautiful, stylized oil paintings accompany the story narrative. Chapter 4—Underground Railroad

Sturges, Philemon. (1998). *Bridges Are to Cross.* New York: G. P. Putnam's Sons. Exquisite colored cut-paper collages provide amazing visual images to accompany Sturges' text. The book invites the reader to examine the myriad types of bridges found around the world. From the Golden Gate Bridge in San Francisco to the Apurimak River suspension bridge in Peru to the curved wooden beam bridge in Japan, the author and illustrator take the reader on an extraordinary journey. Chapter 5—Construction/Architecture

Swamp, Chief Jake. (1997). *Giving Thanks: A Native American Good Morning Message.* New York: Scholastic, Inc. The simple, yet fervent, words of this book are based on a Thanksgiving Address from the Iroquois, or Six Nations, from upstate New York and Canada. Likewise, the full-page color illustrations convey emotion through simplicity. Chapter 4—Cultural Mosaics: Native American

Sweeney, Joan. (1998). *Me on the Map.* New York: Crown Publishers, Inc. A young girl from Kansas describes location through a series of maps. She is in her room, in her home, on her street, in her town, in her state, in her country, on Earth. Brightly colored illustrations include maps that represent each of these contexts. This is an excellent introduction to map making and the uses of maps. Chapter 1—Creating Maps

Takabayaski, Mari. (2001). *I Live in Tokyo.* Boston: Houghton Mifflin Company. Seven-year-old Mimiko leads the reader through a year of life in Tokyo. Organized by the months, beginning with January, the book shares the rich culture of her city. Celebrations, language, food, and fun are revealed through the year. Colorful detailed illustrations have verbal descriptions to help the reader understand the content. Chapter 2—Same and Different Around the World: Asia

Thomas, Joyce Carol. (1998/2000). *I Have Heard of a Land.* New York: Joanna Cotler Books. Lyrical text shouts the hope and courage of pioneers who were willing to journey west. In the late 1800s the Oklahoma Territory was open to everyone, white, black, man, woman. The full-page color illustrations show the reader that this is the story of an African American pioneer woman who is starting a new life of freedom. The author's note describes how her family's westward journey inspired this book. Chapter 4—Westward Expansion.

Tunnell, Michael O. (1997). *Mailing May.* New York: Greenwillow Books. Five-year-old May narrates the story of how she gets to visit her grandma who lives 75 miles away across the Idaho mountains. Based on the true story of Charlotte May Pierstorff, this delightful story shares May's spunk, her father's ingenuity, the challenge of travel, and the delivery of mail in 1914. Ted Rand's full-page watercolor illustrations and clever sepia "photos" enhance the already intriguing story of how May was "mailed" as a baby chick for 53 cents! Chapter 4—Transportation: Land

Turner, Ann. (1998). *Drummer Boy.* New York: HarperCollins Publishers. This is the haunting tale of a 13-year-old boy who feels as if Lincoln's eyes were staring right at him through the crowd, asking him to help the country. So he leaves a note for his dad and, lying about his age, joins the Union army. As a drummer boy, he learns first hand about the sadness of war. The brief, poignant text and the detailed color paintings bring the reader into the life of a young drummer boy. Chapter 4—Civil War

Van Leeuwen, Jean. (1997). *A Fourth of July on the Plains.* New York: Dial Books for Young Readers. Seven-year-old Jesse is frustrated by the limits put on him by others based on his age. Traveling across the plains on the way to Oregon, Jesse's wagon train stops to rest the weary cattle until after the Fourth of July. Finally, as the others are preparing for a holiday, Jessie conceives a wonderful idea for adding to the celebration. The beautiful full-page watercolor, ink, and colored-pencil illustrations enrich the text describing the challenges, hopes, and joys of these pioneers. Chapter 3—Ecosystems: Prairie; Chapter 4—Westward Expansion

Van Leeuwen, Jean. (1998). *Nothing Here but Trees.* New York: Dial Books for Young Readers. A close-knit pioneer family carves out a new home amidst the densely forested land of Ohio in the early 1800s. Beautiful oil and acrylic paintings effectively used as full-page and thumbnail illustrations offer perfect visual accompaniment to the moving text that reminds the reader of the challenges, joys, and hardships of settling the middle part of the United States. Chapter 3—Ecosystems: Other; Chapter 4—Westward Expansion

Van Leeuwen, Jean. (2003). *The Amazing Air Balloon.* New York: Phyllis Fogelman Books. A 13-year-old boy, a blacksmith's apprentice, tells how he became the first American to ride in a balloon. Set in the summer of 1784, this fictionalized story shares facts about the first flight in a balloon built by a little known tavern keeper from a small village outside Baltimore, Peter Carnes. Beautiful oil paintings provide the perfect setting for the excitement of this historic event in Colonial America. A historical note about ballooning is included. Chapter 4—Transportation: Air

Vyner, Tim (2001). *World Team.* Brookfield, CT: Roaring Brook Press. With these words, "One big round world, one small round ball. Right now, more children than you can possibly imagine are playing soccer." The book follows the play and practice of soccer all round the world including boys and girls in Germany, Kenya, Japan, Australia, and India—all tied together with the dreaming of winning the World Cup. Each country and time are marked along the right margin giving a sense of how united we are despite distance and time. The vibrant colors in the illustrations give a sense of place. Chapter 2—Same and Different Around the World: General

Waldman, Neil. (2003). *The Snowflake.* Brookfield, CT: The Millbrook Press. This book takes a unique approach to describing the water cycle. Waldman's exquisite watercolor paintings serve as a backdrop to the journey of a single drop of water through an entire year. As readers watch a single water droplet freeze, melt, evaporate, condense, and then freeze again, they come to a greater understanding of water as a renewable resource that needs to be protected. Chapter 3—Earth's Systems: Nonfiction

Wallner, Alexandra. (2000). *Sergio and the Hurricane.* New York: Henry Holt and Company. Sergio is too young to remember the damage a hurricane can cause, so he's excited when he hears one is coming. Sergio watches as his parents, friends, and neighbors in San Juan, Puerto Rico prepare for the storm. Fortunately, Sergio and his family have only a little damage, but he sees the devastation around him and knows he'll never wish for a hurricane again. Detailed gouache paintings enhance the charming story. Chapter 3—Earth's Systems: Fiction; Chapter 5—Climate/Weather

Weatherby, Brenda. (2004). *The Trucker.* New York: Scholastic Press. One morning Wesley's toy red semi-flatbed rig grew into a full-size 18-wheeler and Wesley had the adventure of a lifetime! Brenda Weatherby's whimsical text, accompanied by her husband, Mark's, multimedia color illustrations tell the dream story of any boy who's longed to drive a big rig. A "trucker talk" glossary is included at the end of the book. Chapter 4—Transportation: Land

Wellington, Monica. (2004). *Crepes by Suzette.* New York: Dutton Children's Books. Suzette, the crepe seller, takes her cart all over the city of Paris. Extraordinary multimedia collages provide the background for Suzette's story. In each scene the customers look familiar because they are based on famous images in fine art such as Cassatt's *Mother and Child.* The author provides a crepe recipe, a French-English glossary, notes on the scenes, and references for the artwork at the end of the book.

Wilkes, Angela. (2001). *A Farm Through Time.* New York: A Dorling Kindersley Book. This extraordinary book follows the life of a farm through 1,200 years from 800 as the land is first cleared and fences and buildings are constructed to the modern farm of 2000. The detailed full-page color illustrations in this oversize book include half-pages revealing additional visual information. The story of the farm through the ages shows the changes in landscape, the unchanging rhythm of the seasons, and the impact of scientific progress. Chapter 6—Layers

Wingate, Phillippa, and Reid, Struan. (2003). *Who Were the First North Americans?* London: Usborne Publishing, Ltd. Using a question-and-answer format, this informational book answers 15 general questions. Some answers are specific to Native American nations and others are rather general. Detailed color illustrations expand the content of the text. Internet links are provided for many of the topics. Chapter 4—Native America

Winnick, Karen B. (2000). *Sybil's Night Ride.* Honesdale, PA: Boyds Mills Press, Inc. Sixteen-year-old Sybil Ludington made a heroic 40-mile ride in the rain on April 26, 1777—two years after Revere's famous April ride. Dressed in breeches, Sybil and her horse, Star, alerted patriots in central Putnam County, New York. Because of Sybil, the patriots were able to push the British back to Long Island Sound. Full-page color illustrations add visual drama to the story. Chapter 4—Revolutionary War

Wong, Janet S. (2000). *The Trip Back Home.* San Diego: Harcourt, Inc. A young girl describes the trip to Korea she makes with her mother to visit her grandparents and aunt. Gentle verbal descriptions matched with detailed watercolor illustrations reveal the joy of family members sharing even when they speak different languages. Chapter 2—Same and Different Around the World: Asia

Woodruff, Elvira. (1999). *The Memory Coat.* New York: Scholastic Press. In this story of a close-knit family of Russian Jews who had to leave their beloved country to escape the tsar's soldiers, cousins Rachel and Grisha hope to make a good impression at Ellis Island so the whole family will be allowed to enter America. In an unexpected accident, it appears that a scratch on Grisha's eyelid may keep him out. Rachel finds a way to use the coat his mother made for him in her last year to work a miracle. The warm text and dramatic oil paintings combine to create a moving story of family, memories, and hopes fulfilled. Chapter 4—Immigration

Woodson, Jacqueline. (2005). *Show Way.* New York: G. P. Putnam's Sons. Woodson's lyrical text tells of her family's tradition passed down from mother to daughter for generations. Each mother taught her daughter how to make "show ways" or quilts which once served as secret maps for freedom-seeking slaves. The extraordinary multimedia illustrations represent a variety of quilt patterns and enhance the story's unique cadence and history. Chapter 4—Underground Railroad

Wright, Betty Ren. (2003). *The Blizzard.* New York: Holiday House. Billy is certain his December birthday will be ruined because of the coming snowstorm that keeps his cousins from the celebration. But much to his surprise, a blizzard arrives that sends all his classmates and the teacher to Billy's house from the one-room school.

Despite the blizzard, Billy has a wonderful celebration. Full-page color paintings complement this warm story of unexpected surprises. Chapter 3—Earth's Systems: Fiction; Chapter 5—Climate/Weather

Wright-Frierson, Virginia. (1996). *A Desert Scrapbook: Dawn to Dusk in the Sonoran Desert.* New York: Simon & Schuster Books for Young Readers. The author-illustrator shares a day in the Sonoran Desert of the American Southwest through a first-person narrative and beautifully detailed watercolors. The focus is this amazing desert setting filled with a vast assortment of flora and fauna able to flourish in the harsh environment. Chapter 3—Ecosystems: Desert

Yezerski, Thomas. (1998). *Together in Pinecone Patch.* New York: Farrar, Straus and Giroux. The people of Ireland and the people of Poland found life to be so difficult in their homeland that many of them immigrated to America. Pinecone Patch, Pennsylvania was a mining town where Irish and Polish families lived in separate neighborhoods. Children were warned about people in the "other" neighborhood. Keara Buckley and Stefan Pazik develop a relationship that affects the entire community. Full-page color illustrations enhance this story that looks at immigrants' lives after they arrive in the new country. Chapter 4—Immigration

Yin. (2000). *Coolies.* New York: Philomel Books. Chinese brothers, Shek and Wong, are engaged in the dangerous work of building the transcontinental railroad in the mid-1800s. Despite the injustice and prejudice that color their treatment, they maintain their cultural traditions. Soentpiet's full-page color paintings are dramatic and complement the emotional story. Chapter 4—Immigration; Land

Yin. (2006). *Brothers.* New York: Philomel Books. In this sequel to *Coolies,* Ming arrives in San Francisco after the long ocean voyage from China to live with his older brothers, Shek and Wong. Although Shek warns Ming not to leave Chinatown where their family store is located, Ming cannot resist. His friendship with Patrick, a kind-hearted Irish boy, opens his world and helps save the family store. Illustrated by the author's husband, Chris Soentpiet, this moving text and beautiful, richly detailed paintings are powerful reminders of the challenges and celebrations of Chinese immigrants in America. Chapter 2—Same and Different Around the World: Asia; Chapter 4—Immigration

Yolen, Jane. (1996). *Encounter.* San Diego: Harcourt Brace & Company. First published in 1992, the 500th anniversary of Columbus's "discovery" of the New World, this story of Columbus looks at the events from another point of view. The text and strong acrylic paintings challenge the reader to think about this historical moment differently. This book would be best used when paired with a traditional telling of the Columbus story. Chapter 4—Exploration

Yolen, Jane. (1996). *Welcome to the Sea of Sand.* New York: G. P. Putnam's Sons. Detailed gouache illustrations and lyrical text describe the beauty and unexpected life of the desert. Set in the Sonoran Desert of Arizona, this book sets to rest the idea that a desert is just sand. Chapter 3—Ecosystems: Desert

Yolen, Jane. (1998). *House, House.* New York: Marshall Cavendish. In the early 1900s, the Howe brothers photographed homes in Hatfield, Massachusetts. A hundred years later, a young Hatfield photographer, Jason Stemple, re-created the photos. Together Yolen and Stemple, mother and son, created this delightful book that places the photos taken 100 years apart on facing pages so the reader can compare then and now. Yolen's text compares life then and now through an examination of economic and social changes. Chapter 6—Layers

Yolen, Jane. (2003). *My Brothers' Flying Machine: Wilbur, Orville, and Me.* New York: Little, Brown and Company. Orville and Wilbur Wright's sister, Katharine, was part of the team. She may not have built the flying machines or flown them, but she was an inspiration. This book tells their story from her point of view. Yolen's lyrical prose and Burke's beautiful oil with colored-pencil paintings join to place the reader in the lives of these three Wright siblings. Chapter 4—Transportation: Air

Zschock, Martha and Heather. (2002). *Journey Around New York from A to Z.* Beverly, MA: Commonwealth Editions. This cleverly organized alphabet book of New York City uses alphabetized alliterative phrases to introduce the unique features of a fascinating city. "Immigrants imagine a better life." introduces the reader to the Statue of Liberty and Ellis Island while "Notes of the *Nutcracker* dance through the night." introduces Lincoln Center and "Tough times take teamwork." describes the heroism connected with September 11, 2001. Detailed color illustrations provide visual complements to the text. A full-page map and locations of the places identified in the text are included at the book's beginning. Chapter 2—Tasting Places in the USA

## Classroom Reference and Informational Books

Asch, Frank. (1998). *Cactus Poems.* New York: Harcourt Brace & Co. Asch's cactus poems are accompanied by wonderful photographs depicting the desert ecosystems in North America that include landforms, flora and fauna. Chapter 3—Ecosystems: Desert

Brooks, Felicity. (1999). *The Usborne First Encyclopedia of Our World.* New York: Scholastic. Detailed color illustrations and easy-to-read text introduce basic concepts of geography. The information is well organized with a table of contents and index to aid the reader. Chapter 1—Atlases

Blanton, Lynne and Hedberg, Betsy. (2003). *States.* Lincolnwood, IL: Publications International, Ltd. This content-rich book about the 50 states is organized by regions, moving from east to west. Information for most states covers two pages, addressing physical, cultural, economic, and political content. Chapter 2—Tour the USA: Informational

Buller, Jon, Schade, Susan, Cocca-Leffler, Maryann, Holub, Joan, Kelley, True, and Regan, Dana. 2003. *Smart about the Fifty States: A Class Report.* New York: Scholastic.

Organized as pages in a class report by intermediate-grade students, this book presents the states alphabetically. Each report provides basic information including the nickname and capital. Cartoon-like drawings of the state and significant people, places, or products fill much of the page. Additional facts are written in more traditional paragraph form. This book is rather informal, but it provides a nice model for classroom teachers to use for students to complete a state report in a brief format. Chapter 2—Tour the USA: Informational

Cheney, Lynne. (2006). *Our 50 States: A Family Adventure Across America.* New York: Simon & Schuster Books for Young Readers. Cheney was inspired by her son-in-law's 10-day trip with his two oldest daughters from Washington, D.C. to Jackson, Wyoming that included special stops along the way. She and illustrator Robin Preiss Glasser have created a rich treasure trove of America's people, places, and history organized by state. The adventure begins in New York and ends in Hawaii. Use the foldout map to help you plan your reading journey through the cleverly organized pages full of small drawings, state maps, and huge amounts of information. Chapter 2—Tour the USA: Informational

Davis, Kenneth C. (2001). *Don't Know Much about the 50 States.* New York: Scholastic, Inc. Each page of this informational book about the 50 states includes the more expected content such as the nickname, capital, flower, bird, and map. It also offers answers to unique questions and an unusual fact that provide interesting insight into the state's history, people, or places. For example: Where in Alaska is it daytime—at night? Or why does Ohio have oodles of apple orchards? Cartoon-like color drawings illustrate this student-friendly resource. Chapter 2—Tour the USA: Informational

DiSpezio, Michael A. (2002). *Map Mania: Discovering Where You Are and Getting to Where You Aren't.* New York: Sterling Publishing Co., Inc. Using cartoon illustration, this informational book provides a rich collection of information about maps and their uses. Ongoing through the book are questions that encourage readers to solve problems based on information in the maps and diagrams. Answers are included. Table of Contents and Index included. Chapter 1—Creating Maps

Hansen, Ole Steen. (2003). *The Story of Flight.* New York: Crabtree Publishing Company. This student-friendly history of flight is divided into six chapters. Each chapter has colored borders, making it easy to access. Color and black-and-white drawings of air vehicles, maps, and diagrams, as well as photographs, provide rich visual support to the informational text. The 190-page book is an excellent classroom reference. Chapter 4—Transportation: Air

Heckscher, Melissa, Shulman, Mark, and the Staff of the Explorer's Gazette. (2004). *The Explorer's Gazette.* New York: Tangerine Press. This unique book contains 30 issues of the *Explorer's Gazette*, each focusing on the accomplishment of a courageous explorer. Each two-page edition provides the headline story and other articles that offer a rich look at the historical, physical, and human aspects of life in the explorer's time.

The first issue documents Alexander the Great's death in 323 B.C.E. Other explorers include Zheng He, Vitus Bering, Richard Byrd, and Voyager I. As the times change and technology improves, the visual aspects of the gazette move from sepia drawings and print to color photographs and updated format. Chapter 4—Exploration

Hopkins, Lee Bennett. (2000). *My America: A Poetry Atlas of the United States.* New York: Scholastic, Inc. Hopkins has assembled an interesting and inspiring collection of poetry organized into eight sections, each reflecting a unique region. In his words, "Through poets' voices our senses are stirred, shaken, awakened to witness the various regions that make up our great United States." Prefacing each section are facts about each state and its capital. Color illustrations of each region join the factual pages and interpret the poetry visually. Chapter 2—Tour the USA: Aesthetic

Hoyt-Goldsmith, Diane. (1997). *Buffalo Days.* New York: Holiday House. This book shares past and present in a conversational narrative that focuses on how the modern-day Crow people live and celebrate their heritage. The Three Irons family who hosted the author and the photographer live on a ranch on the Crow Indian reservation in Montana. Color photos of the people, animals, and land enhance the student-friendly text. Chapter 4—Cultural Mosaics: Native American

Kapp, Billie M. (2006). *Our World: A Child's First Picture Atlas.* Washington, D.C.: National Geographic Society. This atlas is intended for very young children. The basic concepts included are the seven continents, the four oceans bordering them, and the countries on them. Bold colors, easy to read text, photographs, and maps are all developmentally appropriate. Chapter 1—Atlases

Krull, Kathleen. (1997). *Wish You Were Here: Emily's Guide to the 50 States.* New York: A Doubleday Book for Young Readers. Beginning with a two-page color map of the United States indicating the route of the tour of the 50 states, this book contains 50 letters to family about an extraordinary summer trip Emily and her grandmother took. Beginning in New York, the twosome share both human and physical characteristics of each state via the letters. Each two-page spread includes cartoon-like thumbnail paintings of specific locations within the state, as well as a state map locating important cities. Chapter 2—Tour the USA: Informational

Lauber, Patricia. (1998). *Painters of the Caves.* Washington, D.C.: National Geographic Society. This beautiful nonfiction book describes the 1994 discovery of Stone Age rock paintings in a French cave. Lauber's clearly written informational text, accompanied by full-color photographs and other visual data, provides a context for the paintings. She describes the environmental and human conditions at the time they were painted and the importance of this find. Chapter 6—Lesson Plan 6.3

Leedy, Loreen. (1999/2000). *Celebrate the 50 States.* New York: Holiday House. Detailed cartoon-like illustrations provide statistics, cities, and other interesting facts about the 50 U.S. states. The simple format and limited text make this a good resource for primary students learning about their country. Chapter 2—Tour the USA: Informational

Lourie, Peter. (2000). *Mississippi River: A Journey Down the Father of Waters.* Honesdale, PA: Boyds Mills Press. This traditional informational book is organized by the four parts of the 2,340-mile Mississippi River—the headwaters, the upper and lower river, and the delta. Drawings and historical and modern photographs document the text and the author's trip down this mighty river. The informational, yet conversational, narrative make this a great nonfiction addition to any library. Chapter 3—Ecosystems: Rivers

Mann, Elizabeth. (2003). *Empire State Building.* New York: Mikaya Press. This nonfiction book tells the exciting story of this American icon, the Empire State Building. Completed in 1931, the building gained fame and attention because of its speedy construction and extraordinary height, but it found no tenants! It was the beginning of the Great Depression. The informational text is documented by historical photos and some artists' paintings of events. A facts list, glossary, and index are included. Chapter 5—Construction/Architecture

Mappin, Jennifer. (2004). *The Seven Continents of the World Jigsaw Book.* Victoria Australia: The Five Mile Press Pty Ltd. Brightly colored jigsaw puzzles of the continents present a unique way to study Earth's land masses. The seven puzzles are bound together with a plastic sleeve over each one to protect the 48 pieces. The facing page provides basic information and amazing facts about the continent. The puzzle maps contain picture symbols representing indigenous animals, special locations, and products. Chapter 1—Atlases

Morris, Neil. (2005). *Living in the Mountains.* North Mankato, MN: Smart Apple Media. This nonfiction text explores how and why people have made their homes in mountain regions throughout history and around the world. Organized by 12 brief chapters, the information is presented on two-page spreads that include student-friendly text and clear color photographs. A glossary and index are included at the end. Part of a series, other titles include: *Living at the Coast, Living by Rivers, Living by Lakes, Living in Cities,* and *Living on Islands.* Chapter 3—Ecosystems: Mountains

Nadeau, Isaac. (2006). *Mountains.* New York: The Rosen Publishing Group, Inc. This nonfiction text explores the scientific aspects of mountains such as the formation and types of mountains. Organized by 10 brief chapters, the information is presented on two-page spreads that include one page of student-friendly text and the other a full-page color photograph. A glossary and index are included at the end. Part of a series, other titles include: *Canyons, Caves, Glaciers, Islands,* and *Peninsulas.* Chapter 3—Ecosystems: Mountains

Petty, Kate. (2000). *The Amazing Pop-Up Geography Book.* New York: Dutton Children's Books. What child isn't intrigued by a pop-up book? Between the covers of this book are pop-up mountains and volcanoes, lift-the-flap continents and countries, and more. Information about rivers, countries, hurricanes, and people literally jump out of this colorful book. This unique book may be the perfect starting place for a reluctant learner. Chapter 1—Atlases

Pipe, Jim. (2005). *Sun*. Mankato, MN: Stargazer Books. This nonfiction text is an excellent beginning reference book about the sun, our closest star. The content is organized by 13 brief chapters that include information about day and night, the moon, weather and seasons, and energy. Each two-page spread offers student-friendly text and illustrations, diagrams, and/or photographs to enhance the text. A glossary and index are included. Part of a series, other titles include: *Seasons, Water, Weather, My Town, Ecosystems, Our Planet,* and *Getting Around.* Chapter 3—Earth's Systems: Nonfiction

Pirotta, Saviour. (1999). *Rivers in the Rain Forest*. Austin, TX: Raintree Steck-Vaugh Publishers. This nonfiction text introduces aspects of rivers in the rain forest through seven brief chapters following an introduction that locates rain forest on a world map. Each two- to four-page chapter includes student-friendly text and color photographs. An eighth chapter provides clear instructions for readers to create a rainforest canoe from cardboard. A glossary, index, and sources for further reading are included. Part of a series, other titles include: *People in the Rain Forest, Predators in the Rain Forest,* and *Trees and Plants in the Rain Forest.* Chapter 3—Ecosystems: Rain Forest

Robson, Pam. (2005). *My Town*. Mankato, MN: Stargazer Books. This nonfiction text is an excellent reference book for primary students about the development of communities. The content is organized by 13 brief chapters that include information about various size communities, jobs, services, and government. Each two-page spread offers student-friendly text and illustrations, diagrams, and/or photographs to enhance the text. A glossary and index are included. Part of a series, other titles include: *Seasons, Water, Weather, Sun, Ecosystems, Our Planet,* and *Getting Around.* Chapter 2—Chapter 4—Cultural Mosaics

Siebert, Patricia. (2002). *We Were Here: A Short History of Time Capsules*. Brookfield, CT: The Millbrook Press. This informational book organized in chapters examines the modern "time capsule" and how it is similar to and different from other ways humans have left behind evidence of their culture. Included in the book are archive photos of time capsules, Internet sources, suggestions for creating a time capsule, and an index. Chapter 6—Other

Simon, Seymour. (2003). *Earth: Our Planet in Space*. New York: Simon & Schuster Books for Young Readers. This rich nonfiction book about Earth investigates the relationship between our planet, the sun, and the moon. Clearly written text and extraordinary photographs make this an excellent classroom resource. Chapter 3—Earth's Systems: Nonfiction

Simon, Seymour. (2004). *Pyramids & Mummies*. New York: Scholastic. This Simon book has the same eye to detail and awesome photographs we expect in one of his informational books. However, this book is much smaller in size, has less sophisticated language, and is part of Scholastic's See Moor Readers. Chapter 6—Egypt

Sis, Peter. (2004). *The Train of States*. New York: Greenwillow Books. The 50 states of the United States are presented in order of the dates of their statehood from Delaware in 1787 to Hawaii in 1959. Detailed watercolor drawings of train cars include images of indigenous flora and fauna, as well as the state nickname and motto. Other information about each state appears with a unique fact about the state. Notes about the illustrations at the end of the book provide a key to the symbols and encouragement to readers to create their own train of states. Chapter 2—Tour the USA: Informational

Steele, Philip. (2005). *Population Growth.* North Mankato, MN: Smart Apple Media. This nonfiction text examines the impact of population growth on Earth. The rich content is organized by 19 brief chapters and suits students who read at a third-grade level or higher. A glossary, index, and resources for further study are included. Part of a series, other titles include: *Changing Coastlines, The Growth of Cities, Earthquakes & Volcanoes, The Effects of Farming, Rivers in Action; Expanding Industry,* and *Weather & Climate.* Chapter 4—Cultural Mosaics

*Thompson, Gare. (1997). *Immigrants: Coming to America.* New York: Children's Press. "North America is made up of many peoples. All of them came from other places—willingly or unwillingly." This nonfiction text focuses on the various waves of immigration. The content is organized into five chapters that examines the purpose for immigration in time periods 1620–1776, 1776–1860, 1860–1945, and 1945 to the present. Historical photographs and paintings combined with interesting text make this a student series; other titles include: *Cities: The Building of America, Transportation: From Cars to Planes, Leaders: People Who Make a Difference.* Chapter 4—Immigration

*Thompson, Gare. (1997). *Transportation: From Cars to Planes.* New York: Children's Press. "Three inventions, the wheel, sailing ships, and steam engines made transportation possible." With these words, this informational book begins with the development of cars, ships, trains, and airplanes. Simple timelines and informative paragraphs provide an introductory look at the development of transportation. Photographs accompany the text. Part of a *You Are There* series, other titles include: *Cities: The Building of America, Immigrants: Coming to America, Leaders: People Who Make a Difference.* Chapter 4—Transportation

Tunnell, Michael O. and Chilcoat, George W. (1996). *The Children of Topaz: The Story of a Japanese-American Internment Camp.* New York: A Holiday House Book. The authors were inspired to learn more about Topaz after seeing a classroom diary kept by Miss Yamauchi's third grade class at the Topaz Relocation Center in 1943. The text is clearly written and can be read by intermediate-age students. Photographs of diary entries, daily scenes at the camp, and other supporting materials make this a rich source of information about Japanese internment camps. Chapter 4—World War II: Japanese-American Internment Camps

# Teacher Resources

Colman, Penny. (2003). *Girls: A History of Growing Up Female in America.* New York: Scholastic Nonfiction. Colman provides an intriguing look at the history of women growing up in this country. Using a wide variety of primary sources to uncover this story, she shares her discoveries in a conversational narrative. Organized by historical period (colonial to the new millennium), the chapters can be read in or out of order. A summary chronology is printed with the covers, and an index aids the reader seeking specific women or topics.

Dyson, Marianne J. (2003). *Home on the Moon: Living on a Space Frontier.* Washington, D.C.: National Geographic Society. Dyson has loved the moon since she was a child. In fact, her love of and interest in the moon led her to become a physicist, eventually becoming one of the first 10 women to work for NASA in Mission Control. This book is full of interesting facts and historical events related to our knowledge of the moon and Dyson's logic about how this knowledge can support a return to the moon—maybe even set up a moon colony! Photographs and diagrams support the text that is appropriate for grade-three readers and above. Four moon science activities are included in the book. Although much of the content is not directly related to geographic concepts, this book provides excellent background knowledge for teachers to have when teaching geographic concepts about earth/moon relationships. Chapter 3—Earth's Systems: Nonfiction

Johnson, Sylvia A. (1999). *Mapping the World.* New York: Antheneum Books for Young Readers. This text, intended for school-age readers is too complex for K–4 students, but it provides the teacher with a wonderful historical overview of how humans have mapped the world. The tools and techniques used by cartographers have changed as scientific knowledge has grown. A fascinating collection of color maps accompanies the text that demonstrates how our view of the world has changed. Chapter 1—Creating Maps

Littlechild, George. (1993). *This Land Is My Land.* San Francisco: Children's Book Press. Using his own narrative and paintings, Littlechild describes the experiences of Indians of North America in general and his experiences growing up as a Plains Cree Indian in Canada. The provocative text provides insight into living as a marginalized person, as well as insight into the symbolism of the striking color paintings. This is a wonderful resource for teachers and some of the essays would be appropriate for young students as they consider the impact of point of view and "discovering" cultures through exploration. Chapter 4—Cultural Mosaics: Native American

Mochizuki, Ken. (1977). *Passage to Freedom: The Sugihara Story.* New York: Lee & Low Books, Inc. Five-year-old Hiroki Sugihara, the eldest son of the Japanese consul to Lithuania, saw hundreds of Jewish refugees from Poland who had come to ask Hiroki's father to issue them visas to escape the Nazis. Set in 1940, based on Hiroki Sugihara's own words, this is a story of remarkable courage. Dramatic illustrations complement this extraordinary narrative. Although less sophisticated than other stories of Nazi oppression of the 1940s, this book may not be appropriate for young children, but it certainly provides a great background resource for the teacher. Chapter 4—World War II

Rosen, Matthew T. (1999). *The Handy Geography Answer Book.* Canton, MI: Visible Ink Press. This paperback volume has a vast amount of easily accessed information for the reader. The first 20 chapters are organized by topics in geography such as water and ice, climate, political geography, and explorations, as well as regions of the world. Knowledge is dispersed via questions and answers that are posed and resolved within the chapters. The 21st chapter lists the 192 countries of the world and their key statistics. An extensive index and maps appear at the end of the book.

Rubin, Susan Goldman. (2001). *Fireflies in the Dark: The Story of Friedl Dicker-Brandeis and the Children of Terezin.* New York: Scholastic, Inc. This brief, but powerful chapter book honors the memory of Friedl Dicker-Brandeis who was "resettled" in Terezin, a camp for Jews during World War II. A painter, designer, teacher, and art therapist in her days of freedom, Friedl was assigned to work with children in the camp. The story of her service and life in Terezin was reconstructed through diaries and interviews. The book includes photos and children's drawings. An extensive reference list and index are at the end of the book. Chapter 4—World War II

Say, Allen. (1999). *Tea with Milk.* Boston: Houghton Mifflin Company. May is raised in California by her parents who speak Japanese at home and prefer rice and miso soup and green tea. May likes the pancakes and fried chicken she eats at her friends' houses and plans to go to college and have her own apartment. When her parents move the family back to Japan, May feels like a "gaijin," a foreigner where everyone calls her by her Japanese name and she has to wear a kimono and sit on the floor. She finally sets out to find her own way in the big city of Osaka. Say's story of his mother and her struggle belonging to two cultures is touching. The beautiful, detailed watercolors are a perfect accompaniment to his parents' path to finding their true home. Chapter 2—Same and Different Around the World: Asia; Chapter 4—Immigration

Say, Allen. (2002). *Home of the Brave.* Boston: Houghton Mifflin Company. This haunting story is told in dreamlike sequences as a man symbolically confronts the trauma of incarceration in an internment camp. Say's beautiful paintings provide a visually haunting complement to the text. Certainly too abstract and mature for most K–4 students, this book is important for teachers to read to consider past injustices and strive for a future of equality. Chapter 4—World War II: Japanese-American Internment Camps

Shulevitz, Uri. (2005). *The Travels of Benjamin of Tudela: Through Three Continents in the Twelfth Century.* New York: Farrar Straus Giroux. In 1159, Benjamin left his native town of Tudela in northern Spain to begin a 14-year journey through most of the then-known world. Such travels, more than 100 years before Marco Polo, were extraordinary. Full-page color illustrations accompany the first-person fictionalized narrative. Although this text is not as student-friendly as Rumford's tale of a fourteenth-century traveler, Benjamin is an adventurer/explorer worthy of note. Chapter 4—Exploration

Weatherford, Carole Boston. (2006). *Moses: When Harriet Tubman Led Her People to Freedom.* New York: Hyperion Books for Children. In lyrical text, Weatherford tells the story of Harriet Tubman's spiritual journey as she hears the voice of God guiding her to freedom. Harriet Tubman was a slave who, after she achieved freedom for herself, became the famous conductor on the Underground Railroad. This beautifully illustrated book is a unique and moving portrait of this intriguing heroine. Teachers will need to assess how appropriate the religious overtones are for the classroom when making a decision about sharing it with students. Chapter 4—Underground Railroad

# Index

# About the Author

DR. LINDA K. ROGERS is an associate professor of education at East Stroudsburg University in Pennsylvania and author of a previous Teacher Ideas Press book, *Geographic Literacy Through Children's Literature* (1997).

**DATE DUE**